1997

University of St. Francis
GEN 321.8 B402

Teaching democracy by being de

W9-AOX-132

TEACHING DEMOCRACY BY BEING DEMOCRATIC

Praeger Series in
Transformational Politics and Political Science

The Politics of Transformation: Local Activism in the Peace and Environmental Movements
Betty H. Zisk

The Latino Family and the Politics of Transformation
David T. Abalos

Mediation, Citizen Empowerment, and Transformational Politics
Edward W. Schwerin

Strategies of Transformation Toward a Multicultural Society: Fulfilling the Story of Democracy
David T. Abalos

Beyond Confrontation: Transforming the New World Order
Charles Hauss

TEACHING DEMOCRACY BY BEING DEMOCRATIC

Edited by Theodore L. Becker
and Richard A. Couto

Foreword by James MacGregor Burns

Praeger Series in Transformational Politics
and Political Science
Theodore L. Becker, Series Adviser

LIBRARY
College of St. Francis
JOLIET, ILLINOIS

PRAEGER

Westport, Connecticut
London

Library of Congress Cataloging-in-Publication Data

Teaching democracy by being democratic / edited by Theodore L. Becker
  and Richard A. Couto ; foreword by James MacGregor Burns.
      p.   cm.—(Praeger series in transformational politics and
  political science, ISSN 1061-5261)
    Includes bibliographical references and index.
    ISBN 0-275-95552-4 (alk. paper). —ISBN 0-275-95553-2 (pbk.)
    1. Democracy—Study and teaching—United States. 2. College
  student government—United States. 3. Student volunteers in social
  service—United States. 4. Community and college—United States.
  5. Universities and colleges—United States—Public services.
  I. Becker, Theodore Lewis. II. Couto, Richard A.
  III. Series.
  JC423.T33   1996
  321.8'071'173—dc20   96–20930

British Library Cataloguing in Publication Data is available.

Copyright © 1996 by Theodore L. Becker and Richard A. Couto

All rights reserved. No portion of this book may be
reproduced, by any process or technique, without the
express written consent of the publisher.

Library of Congress Catalog Card Number: 96–20930
ISBN: 0-275-95552-4
       0-275-95553-2 (pbk.)
ISSN: 1061–5261

First published in 1996

Praeger Publishers, 88 Post Road West, Westport, CT 06881
An imprint of Greenwood Publishing Group, Inc.

Printed in the United States of America

The paper used in this book complies with the
Permanent Paper Standard issued by the National
Information Standards Organization (Z39.48–1984).

10 9 8 7 6 5 4 3 2 1

321.8
B402

Contents

158, 401

Foreword

James MacGregor Burns

Not long ago I had the kind of experience that *Teaching Democracy by Being Democratic* illuminates. Some colleagues and I, concerned about the non-representation or underrepresentation of huge groups of Americans in Congress, convened a gathering of grass-roots or "cobblestone" leaders of such groups. Women, African Americans, ex-offenders, "illegal" aliens, Native Americans, and others accepted our invitation. Absent were teen-age representatives of the largest of nonrepresented groups in Congress—children.

My colleagues and I were aware that our leadership in calling this gathering gave us no commanding role in the discussion that followed. We had agreed that we would merely start the meeting off and let the invited participants take over. Still, we felt we needed to state the assumptions that lay behind the gathering. But immediately some of those assumptions were challenged. Why did we take for granted that they *wanted* representation in an irremediably "elitist" government? Why representation in *Congress*, that hopelessly reactionary institution? Why try to begin a debate that would be inevitably muffled or distorted by the media? And where were the children?

Most of all—and to our considerable surprise—the participants challenged our assumption that we had some right or duty to convene this meeting, because, inevitably, this assumption would color the nature of the discussion. Who were we to do this? In vain we contended that we were "only getting things started." A long discussion followed as the group shifted the subject to *their* assumptions. The outcome was best expressed by one of the African-American participants: "You called this meeting hoping we would join *you*—we will go ahead and let you join *us*."

This incident illustrated one of the most daunting problems in the study of leadership. That study has come a long way, of course, since the old-time emphasis on the "man-on-the-white-horse"—almost always a white man on that horse—approach to leadership. Now we think in more sophisticated psychological and political terms about the intricate symbiotic relationship between would-be leaders and their targets. Someone—the leader—must take some originating action to set in motion the leadership-followership interaction. But the originator does so—assuming a desire to attract a follower—by estimating the wants, needs, expectations, or political attitudes of the follower. In that interaction, who is really the leader and who is really the follower?

All this also applies to the task of teaching democracy by being democratic, for the teacher-student relationship is at heart a leader–potential leader–relationship. Just as leaders ideally lead "followers" in such a way that the followers become the leaders' leaders, so teachers teach students in such a way that the learners become the teachers' teachers. To our infinite joy, we teachers have all seen this happen. I can think of many students whom I once mentored and who now mentor me.

This volume, with its concern for community organization, students as collaborators, personal empowerment, the "community of need and response," and democratic organization, was written with a knowing eye for modern leadership theory. But it also links this theory to practice. Teachers and other readers will learn much about tested techniques in teaching democracy by being democratic in the classroom. The authors do not sentimentalize or idealize—they are tough minded about what works and what fails to work. They are creative themselves in calling for imagination in the classroom, as in their concluding chapter on the Televote.

Other approaches and techniques are detailed in this rich offering. They include structuring a democratic classroom; democratic practices that empower students; problem solving and community service that make the classroom a laboratory for democracy; and university-based programs of democratic alternatives that serve the community.

Still, in the end, we have the dilemma of the trigger or spark that sets off leading and responding, teaching and learning. *Someone* must get things started, whether in a classroom or in an election campaign. The authors have taken leadership in writing this volume—but in a way that will create legions of new teachers and leaders in the classroom.

Acknowledgments

We are indebted to several people who helped us in very specific ways to produce this book. Our contributors met deadlines and dealt with suggestions for revisions generously. Arlene Belzer, our production editor, ferreted out our errors of omission and commission and clarified the expression of many ideas in the book. The University of Richmond Faculty Research Committee provided support for copying and mailing manuscripts. The Kellogg Leadership Studies Project provided Couto a rich context for thought and discussion. Charlotte Chandler and Judy Mable processed the manuscript and found elusive files on errant diskettes when necessary. Ashley Broom and Anna Johnson helped in the last stage of manuscript preparation. They brought "fresh eyes" and meticulous detail to the task of proofreading.

In a general way, we are indebted to the thousands of students and dozens of colleagues who taught us by word and example. We dedicate this book to them.

Inbetween these specific and general contributions are those of Dan Eades, our intrepid editor. His vision helped initiate the Praeger Series on Transformational Politics and Political Science. His commitment sustains it and made this book possible.

TEACHING DEMOCRACY BY BEING DEMOCRATIC

Introduction

Theodore L. Becker and Richard A. Couto

As long as there has been democracy on this planet, we can safely assume that adult human beings have attempted to pass knowledge about it on to their young in some combination of theory and practice. But as is true with any theory-practice relationship, the devil is in the details. So, we can also assume that as long as people have taught democracy, they have thought about and quarreled over the best way to combine theory and practice. This book offers thoughts about teaching democracy and joins in the quarrel over the best way to do that.

Teaching democracy is like teaching anything else, that is: You have to justify *why* the topic is important—philosophy and theory; You have to explain *what* the topic is and how it has evolved over time—history; You need to offer knowledge about *how* to teach it—pedagogy. Unlike most books about teaching democracy, this one spends more time on *how* to teach democracy and *how* to teach it democratically. The Introduction explains *what* and *why*. The rest of the book explains that teaching democracy involves doing democracy and being democratic.

DIRECT AND INDIRECT DEMOCRACY

Unlike teaching other topics, the teaching of democracy presents a special problem because of the wide parameters of what is meant by "democracy." It is commonplace, for example, for even the most autocratic tyrant to call a system of governance a "people's democracy." Even when the term *democracy* is applied correctly, there is a wide and legitimate variation in this form of self-government. For example, the difference is apparent between direct and indirect democracy, the latter often being called a republic in which the people theoretically lend their right and power to make the laws to a small group of citizens whom they select through some sort of election. These so-called representatives of the people are then charged with the job of making the laws for the rest of society.

Some critics of representative democracy claim that it can never work as advertised. From this perspective, once the citizens yield their power to directly decide the policies of their state, they have, at that instant, surrendered the freedom to rule themselves. The famous French philosopher, Jean-Jacques Rousseau, put it like this: "Law being purely the declaration of the general will, it is clear that, in the exercise of the legislative power, the people cannot be represented. . . . In any case, the moment a people allows itself to be represented, it is no longer free: it no longer exists" (Rousseau 1950:xv).

Other critics of representative democracy say that the very concept is an oxymoron. They point out that no representative democracy has ever closely represented the full range of its citizenry. Its true nature has been—and must be—to overrepresent the wealthy, educated, aggressive, and articulate segments of the society, a group that is a tiny fraction of the populace. Thomas Jefferson expressed this criticism when he urged direct democracy at the ward level. If indirect democracy was inevitable at the national level, then direct democracy was all the more necessary at the local level, and national politics had to be decentralized to a size where direct democracy could occur.

Most contemporary democratic theorists strongly disagree with these criticisms of representative democracy. Instead, they claim that there is no conceivable way that the citizens of huge, modern nation-states could possibly take the time and effort necessary to establish laws. The vast number of citizens are not able to acquire crucial information and do not have the time to deliberate the pros and cons of alternative laws, not possessing the inclination to do either anyway. Supporters of representative democracy also argue that even if the representatives are a highly selective group—in terms of their socioeconomic background and personal characteristics—this does not keep them from passing laws that are for the good of all, that serve a broader set of interests. Even Rousseau agreed that his theory best applied to small, compact countries, like Switzerland.

Thus, today's predominant form of democracy throughout the Northern Hemisphere and in some parts of the Southern Hemisphere as well, is the republic—with an elected executive and with legislative bodies responsible for the will of the people and, theoretically, accountable to them mainly through the mechanism of regular elections. This theory also posits that there are intermediaries, like the mass media and political parties, that filter information about public sentiment and opinion to the government and back to the people about what the government intends to do and what it actually does. The role of the citizen is to keep abreast of what is occurring and to participate via voting, supporting a political party, belonging to organized political associations, and so forth.

Indirect democracy has vestiges of direct democratic institutions, whereby citizens actually make key decisions themselves, not through representatives. Most European nations, for example, allow for national referenda on major policy and process issues, and Switzerland has two forms of citizens' initiatives as well. The United States has neither the referenda nor initiatives at the national level, but both exist throughout the nation at the state and local level. Also, town meetings exist in parts of New England and citizen-staffed juries are guaranteed to American citizens in major criminal trials.

Other vestiges of direct democracy in American political culture are found in community organizations. These organizations have historically gone under a variety of names. De Tocqueville commented on them as voluntary associations. President George Bush referred to them as "1,000 points of light." Whatever their names, a segment of contemporary community organizations serve to continue an American political tradition of direct citizen action in public problem solving. A problem rises, however, as to whether the organization itself is run democratically or hierarchically, with very few fitting into the former paradigm. Thus, we have the contradiction of direct, democratic action working within undemocratic, or even antidemocratic, bureaucratic settings.

Democracy, whether direct or indirect, empowers the ordinary citizen to be responsible for public policy. This implies a complicated set of responsibilities as a complement to the power. The citizen should be informed about what is occurring; should deliberate on the state of public affairs in general and on specific issues; should listen to a wide variety of views of other citizens; and should act in the best interests of the nation in general. Thus, it is not easy to be a good citizen in a democracy. In fact, it is a heavy burden, but it is shed only at the risk of becoming an oppressed subject in a tyrannical dictatorship or an acquiescent actor in inequitable oligarchies.

James MacGregor Burns has identified a paradox entailed in this risk. Democracy enables the transformation of leadership not by leaders but by the relationship of leaders and followers. It provides for increased levels of human capacities and possibilities only if ordinary citizens convince their leaders to assist them in reaching these levels. The heavy burden of citizenship includes providing direction for leaders. Because of this two-way relationship of leaders and followers, democracy, whether direct or indirect, requires the active participation of citizens as both leaders and followers.

TEACHING POLITICS TO THE YOUNG

Whatever the system of politics—from the most democratic to the least, from the most primitive to the most complicated, from the most hierarchical and despotic to the most egalitarian and humane—the same elements of education will appear: the philosophy, history, and alleged benefits of that particular political system. Information will be delivered to the young orally and, if the system is literate, via the written word as well. Additionally, we can be certain that what is taught will carry a strong bias toward procreating the eccentricities of that particular political system—its ideology, its DNA, its operating manual. How could it be otherwise? What system works against its own highly egocentric and eccentric sense of stability and order?

Totalitarian dictatorships are particularly good at teaching politics because they realize that the right political lessons keep citizens in check, teach them to bow and scrape, and permit the rulers to rule with minimal resistance and maximum deference. They are extremely systematic in their passion to inculcate the values of their system into the young, routinely developing highly organized programs of overt indoctrination. Such educational systems emphasize a fawning loyalty to the ruling class and the folly of not slavishly following its orders. Thus, the Nazis—as putative saviors of the Aryan race and its destiny—cloned their Hitler Jungen, and the Communist Party of the Soviet Union—as the self-styled "vanguard of the proletariat"—manufactured its Young Pioneers. Since each regime was ultramilitaristic, these educational programs were superregimented, uniform, and uniformed.

More authentic democratic political systems have entirely different educational missions since their philosophies embrace such ideas and ideals as free thought, free speech, and the importance of individualism. These systems emphasize the key role of the individual citizen in the running of government and the equality of each citizen—one person, one vote. Theoretically, in democracy, there is no such thing as unquestioned leadership and a ruling elite. Personal responsibility for civic matters is emphasized, as is the right—if not the duty—to dissent. This holds equally as true in representative democracies as it does in direct democratic systems. Implicitly, teaching democracy also entails encouraging students to question authority, including the teacher's, and to dissent appropriately, that is, as a citizen of the classroom. These are steps beyond the fostering of inquiring minds and critical thinking. They involve teaching students to act democratically so as to promote democracy, the process.

TEACHING DEMOCRACY: PRELITERATE TIMES

People have been teaching democracy ever since they have been democratic. In fact, the first method used to teach the young how to be democratic was probably one which we, as dwellers in an age of high technology and megaexpertise, would dub "experiential education."

After all, what were the first democratic societies? According to our best guesses as to how people governed themselves in prehistoric days, there existed some relationship between hunter-gatherer societies and self-governance. Since there were no written records among such peoples, they taught by word of mouth and by showing children how things were done. For example, what was the best way to sneak up on tonight's steak dinner? ("Here's how.") Which berries tasted sweet and which were a sure bet for cramps? ("Don't eat those red ones.") How could a weakling best heave a lance against the wind? ("Aim low.") And who was going to tell the chieftain that his idea about moving out only a few days before the rains was risky business? ("Okay, folks, let's all gather 'round, talk it over and decide who's going to tell him.")

That final question was bound to raise another, more fundamental question. Sooner or later, some pesky kids—not unlike our students today—would ask: What kinds of decisions were made by the chief? What kinds by the whole band? Who decided who decides what? How did the group ordinarily go about making decisions? The way the young learned answers to these and other questions was by being told and initiated into well-established decision-making processes.

Teaching had to be done this way. By definition, hunter-gatherer societies were close knit and always on the move, with their survival always in jeopardy. There was little time for reflection on metaphysical questions on the nature and constitution of authority. They had a modest margin for error. The youth of these societies, unlike our students, had to assume all major responsibilities as quickly as they could. On-the-hunt training was essential. In some cases, so was ad hoc, oral self-governance. Technical education dominated these early forms of democracy. The acquisition of skills best assured the economic security of the group.

TEACHING DEMOCRACY: ANCIENT TIMES

As the human species developed, societies became defined by borders and became more or less self-sufficient via agriculture. Individual lives and functions also became more separated and specialized. With the advent of writing and recordkeeping, the educational enterprise shifted gradually from learning in the field through personal experiences to learning in some kind of structured setting from other people's experience. Teachers taught more by talking about how to do something than from actually doing it. By and large, theory superseded practice. Lecturing, writing, and dialogue came to dominate apprenticeship—particularly regarding such important theoretical matters as theology, philosophy, and politics. The economic security of the group permitted a few adventurous educators to move beyond the technical tradition to a humanistic tradition. Teachers and students could speculate on the potential of human beings, their institutions, and their practices, including those of their governments.

Occasionally a more developed society was open enough to discuss, and even practice, some form of democratic process. Some early Greek city-states come to mind as does the limited Roman citizenry that also elected a wide array of powerful officials. As far as we know, the children in these places did not serve as official "interns" in the citizen assemblies, and they certainly did not vote as participants. Mostly, they learned about their system of democracy from teachers. They learned the ideology, the theory, and the historical context of their political process.

Perhaps one of the greatest teachers of democracy in this humanist tradition was Socrates. After all, in its purest form, the Socratic method of dialogue between teacher and students invites students to question assumptions—including those about authority—and to then deal with the flaws in these assumptions, their own thought processes, as well as the inadequacies of their views of reality. This could well lead to dissent from views routinely implanted by those in positions of authority over the child, for example, parents and tutors. An inquiring mind and critical faculties are clearly important tools that any citizen must hone in order to be effective in a genuinely democratic system. The primary safeguard of democracy resides in the ability of citizens to question and to dissent from authority. Thus, the pure Socratic dialectic, or even some watered-down version of it, belongs in any pedagogical toolbox used to teach democracy by being democratic.

Of course, those who want to pattern their teaching method after that of Socrates also must realize that his method offended many of those in power. Sharpening the critical capacities of the children of any elite group is a dangerous game for teachers to play. What rich patricians want to hear their sons or daughters question their right to rule? What senators want to be challenged by their offspring as to how they voted to support military forays into the hinterlands? What "normal" citizens want to hear their own offspring say that the basic values of their society are inconsistent, hypocritical, and/or self-destructive? When teachers of democratic skills become famous among the populace for successfully teaching students to question, how long will it be before the powerful, in defense of democracy, find just cause to expel, excommunicate, or exterminate them for "corrupting the youth"?

With Socrates as the prime example of what happens to effective democratic teachers in self-congratulatory, quasi-democratic states, it is not too surprising to find human history skipping many centuries before one finds anything about teaching the theory and practice of democracy. Where on earth did it exist from the Romans through the European Dark and Middle Ages? Not in the Middle East. Not anywhere in Asia. Not among the Incas or Aztecs. Not in Africa.

Yes, there were still some primitive people whose hunting and gathering economies helped them to maintain a democratic way of life. There were definite islands of democracy in North America among some of the Native American tribes. Perhaps the most celebrated example of this was in the Iroquois nation, where numerous democratic practices caught the attention of some enlightened American political theorist-practitioners like Thomas

Jefferson and Benjamin Franklin (Johansen 1982). Another example of democracy was seen in some of the Maori tribes in New Zealand, where decision making was based on a town-meeting concept of the "marai."

TEACHING DEMOCRACY IN EARLY AND MODERN REPUBLICAN TIMES

But democracy, in the Western, modern sense, did not begin to make its appearance until the coming of the Enlightenment in Europe, when a host of philosophical advances coalesced—along with important technological revolutions of the time—to supersede the centuries-old domination of anthropomorphic theocracies, hereditary plutocracies, and inbred monarchies. The progeny of the landed aristocrats had to begin to share their education with the prodigal sons of the newly emergent, bourgeois elite and to begin to comprehend the complex philosophies and theories that justified and legitimated these fledgling "republican," indirect, and democratic forms of governance.

With the educational system still substantially grounded in religious institutions and directed by the hirelings of the well bred and well fed, the format and style of education was still very much elitist, hierarchical, authoritarian, and about as undemocratic in delivery and communication as possible. In addition, these representative democracies were, in truth, nothing more than a merger of an old and new elite that simply had to devise new methods to maintain control of the rabble: the ignorant, the nasty, the slothful masses who grew their food, built their mansions, forged their tools, and waged their wars. The political-economic system the new elites were developing and passing on to their children was that of "mercantilism"— an alliance between the governmental-landholding elites and the new financial-commercial elites. They, together, controlled the state apparatus, with the major goal being to increase the wealth of nations via developing favorable trade balances with the rest of the world. The best route to this cornucopia traversed the mastering of cluster "colonies"—a euphemism for militarily appropriated land and natural resources and the forced labor of subjugated people.

The educational system in these representative democracies taught the youngsters of the new elite the essentials of social control: How to read, count, rationalize and praise the history of their new system, as well as how to handle the reins of governing in the name of, and with the presumed consent of, the people of their respective countries. Because such an education was initially privately financed, only the children of those with surplus money could afford it. The vast majority of people, at this time, enrolled their children in the day-to-day struggle to get by. They could not afford to pay for an education for their children. In addition, they needed their sons and daughters to help them eke out their livings and stave off dying from a wide array of diseases and injuries. The educational system in these newly minted representative democracies was largely, if not exclusively, the province of the economic elites—which made them, ipso facto, the ruling class. Under the theory of early representative democratic governments, only they were mentally and morally fit to captain the ship of state anyway.

But what of those who were supposed to select them, that is, the propertied, male electorate? If most of this group couldn't obtain a formal education, how could they know what was going on so they could discuss, think, and vote with some knowledge and comprehension of the issues and candidates? They used what some have called the popular education tradition to learn—just as people before them had done when frozen out of the formal, elitist educational system. They used their distance from those institutions as a textbook about them and on their social, political, and economic position. The slaves, women, indentured servants, debtors, subcitizens, and other underclasses of Greece, Rome, Europe, and America understood they had no access to the superior rank of citizen. Their technical education, supplied by the wealthy landowners and industrialists, supported an economy premised on their subordinate economic standing and political passivity. However, their own popular education supported their sense of justice and their hope for expanded human rights and truly democratic practices.

Throughout most of human history, popular education in the modern representative democracies has been severely limited. Although most ordinary workers, farmers, and others couldn't read, they could listen to speeches and talk among themselves. They could also become informed by those among them who could read and who did have some formal education. And they could see and feel what government was doing for them and to them. Moreover, during the agricultural and early industrial phases of representative democracy, the educated elites who occupied important governmental posts lived—and sometimes even worked—among although not with—the general population. Thus, there was some direct communication between the ruling elite and the people about their respective viewpoints and problems. This exchange provided ordinary people with useful information but also permitted the elites to check out the Socratic "rabble-rousers" of the popular education tradition.

The new philosophy of reason, the basis for the new representative democracies, required new ways to rationalize the power and position of the ruling elites in addition to keeping in check the popular tradition. The prevalent practice of the time that limited the voting citizenry exclusively to those who owned real estate was justified by the notion that owning land gave a person a stake in society and, therefore, sufficient motivation to mull over affairs of state, that is, to be able to dwell in the realm of politics and to be abundantly concerned about it. Sharecroppers, indentured servants, craftsmen, newcomers, and their ilk supposedly did not have ample material interests and thus would not have the incentive to become involved seriously in public affairs. Additionally, they did not have the pecuniary wherewithal to gain the level of formal education prerequisite to civic virtue, that is, a surplus of leisure time to read and think about such lofty subjects as foreign affairs, monetary policy, and sin taxes.

It was not until the Industrial Revolution had soared to an entirely new height of development that universal literacy and a more advanced knowledge base for the general population seemed to be essential for the continued expansion of the national economies of states. With international and interstate trade booming and with mass-production assembly lines becoming the dominant engines of capital growth, there was more need for people who could keep books and records, read instructions, and grasp the complex tasks involved in running equipment and working in groups.

This need produced an understanding among the governing and economic elites that there had to be greater access to primary, secondary, and higher education for much larger and broader segments of the population than theretofore was considered necessary or possible. Some educators had long called for expanded access, but it was not until the economic elites saw the need for it to spur further economic growth that the public education movement—from grade school through college—took root and began to flourish.

This movement began the liberal tradition of American education, a tradition that provided much more access to formal education, but that also emphasized social, political, and economic functions divided and organized by race, gender, and class. Being a state-run system in a free-enterprise economy, it promoted such values as individualism, materialism, and competition while also inculcating personal deference to authority figures like parents, teachers, business owners, and the government.

Of course, some liberal educators and thinkers had also seen the connection between a more vibrant form of representative democracy and free and mandatory public education for quite some time before it became available. From their viewpoint, what some know as the progressive tradition, the importance of education was less related to molding workers for the next stage of the Industrial Revolution than it was to preparing individual people to work together for a more significant and meaningful role in cultural development and self-governance. In the world-view of such progressive educators, publicly supported education—even through college and professional schools—would lead to a more dynamic society and to more creative grass-roots politics, with the new bottom-up surge blossoming into a more prosperous and just society. Nevertheless, it still took a great deal of time to establish more universal public education at all levels.

MAJOR POLITICAL FUNCTIONS OF MODERN DEMOCRATIC EDUCATION

Aside from the plans of the industrial elites and the theories of educators, what are the actual political functions of the modern—public and private—democratic educational systems in the United States and in all modern representative democracies? Since only about 20 percent of the youth of any society percolate up to sample college or university life, most of the political functions of public education take place in the K-12 grade range. Of course, other equally or even more important functions are performed at the college level and in schools of law, medicine, and other professions.

Perhaps the major political goal of this entire system is to move some outstanding members of the lower classes—middle, working, poor, and underclass—up to positions of economic and political power. Thus, a quasi-meritocracy has emerged over time, melding the children of traditional and monied elites with the best, brightest, and most ambitious offspring of the other, lower classes and reinforcing the enduring but permeable nature of class boundaries that, in modern times, is the quintessential feature of the class system's resistance to change. After all, permeable but enduring class boundaries permit the vision—"The American Dream," "The Saga of Sam Walton," and so forth—that anyone, but not everyone, can become powerful if they understand the rules, play by them, and work hard at climbing the ladder to the top. This vision of wealth and power is the most seductive and most widely played lottery system ever devised by human brainpower.

Those who are born into privilege and wealth are taught the attitudes, skills, and manners to maintain the political and economic power to which they are heirs, that is, their established niche, within the governing class. Many of this class decide to continue in those roles and do so successfully. Those who are not born into this class have varying opportunities to gain access to positions in which they can work for and/or with the elite. The closer one gets to the higher levels of power, the shorter the distance one must travel to get there and the easier it is to travel the educational system that is the road to political position and privilege. Despite these long odds, the appeal of the system is that most Americans who reach the top 1 percent in income and wealth did not start there. Recent data indicate that of those currently in what might be called the American economic elite, 40 percent achieved their fortune by inheritance while 60 percent arrived at the top by starting small businesses, rising through the corporate ranks, or by being extremely successful in one of the professions.

In any event, one can see limited access to the top rung of the economic ladder as an ingenious device whereby the modern public-private educational system in representative democracies simultaneously reinforces and democratizes the governing class in representative governments. This access strengthens the ruling class by adding new pools of talent and makes it appear to represent all ethnic groups and socioeconomic backgrounds. The net result is the creation of what some political scientists have called "democracy for the few" (Parenti 1983) or governance by "democratic elites" (Dye and Ziegler 1996), that is, a government of elites, by elites, and for elites, albeit in the name of the people.

CURRENT DEMOCRATIC EDUCATIONAL PRACTICE

In order to see the restrictions on democratic ideals and practice, we need to analyze the structure, content, and delivery of modern republican educational systems. By way of example, let us take a look at the omnipresent classroom structure in the American school system. At the elementary school level, there is almost no democracy to be found in the entire educational enterprise. The system is almost completely autocratic. With rare exceptions: (1) administration is top-down; (2) the curriculum is tightly controlled; and (3) the teacher is the dictatorial purveyor of orthodox, politically neutral, and/or correct information in the classroom. Moreover, as the social and economic systems continue to unravel, public school teachers find themselves being placed into the role of policemen, desperately trying to discipline their wards. Nevertheless, both inside and outside the classroom, teachers in the American primary and secondary system who dare to criticize approved texts or deviate from conventional political thinking will not stay long. Teachers are unchallenged in the schools as long as they don't challenge the theory and/or practices of the modern American political economy.

Indeed, the preeminent purpose of public school education is technical—to teach the three Rs and to discipline and regiment the minds of those who will toil in the factories, fields, and service industries, serve as enlisted personnel in the military, and choose contentedly among a narrow range of options prepared by political and economic elites. Only a small percentage of students are "tracked" into college and university life where they will receive further technical training to improve the external and internal efficiency of social-economic institutions and organizations premised on the so-called natural order: economic inequality and limited democracy. Those from the nonruling classes will be "re-*class*-ified" as potential members of the governing elite.

The content of political education in both the private and public sectors strongly reinforces the ideology of the value of control by a democratic elite. First, it relies heavily on a history purified by market ideology. Critics of the twists and turns of American history have made some inroads in recent years. However, the overwhelming message behind the teaching of American history and politics remains overwhelmingly praiseworthy—despite some reluctantly admitted problems and excesses—and that the American system is by far the best ever devised by humankind. The main focus is placed on the contributions of elites, from the Founding Fathers—who are portrayed as demigods—through a parade of presidents, military men, statesmen, and major manufacturing moguls. Thus, the main thrust of American political education is to persuade most students to accept their role in the continuation of a mythical past as mere citizens beholden to a few great leaders whom they are unlikely to join.

At the kindergarten through high school levels, the content of education concerning the process of modern government also teaches passivity. First, there is precious little education about democratic government. Second, what has traditionally been taught about American government has a strong bias that is conducive to maintaining it in its present form, that is, highly conservative. For example, the emphasis in almost all civics courses taught in modern-day America is on the process of elections and legislation. This puts average students in their proper places, that is, as voters and as spectators of the game established political actors play. Almost nothing is ever presented to American students to encourage them to participate more directly in advocating and implementing policies they support or demonstrating against policies they oppose; in learning how to establish citizens' initiatives and referendums; or in understanding the importance of citizens' rights and the government—the history, text, and practice of the Bill of Rights.

The small group entering college through their families' resources, public financing, or private scholarships, receives more information about passive citizenship in their history and political science courses. The values, data and interpretation of the political system—historically and at present—are akin to that which is relayed to the other 80 percent of the citizenry virtually excluded from public office by virtue of having only a high school—or less—education. After all, most of them have little to no intention of ever running for public office themselves or becoming hot-shot financial magnates or Fortune-500 CEOs. They are usually required to take one such course that is either the first they have ever taken or that simply embellishes that which they were compelled to take in high school.

The precious few of this future elite who want to move into the exalted ranks of political and/or economic control or management usually gear their studies toward law, business management, or political science—the ancient technical tradition revived in the form of professional preparation. Only this group begins to learn the intricacies of the system of political-economic control and the subtleties of the theory and ideology that supports it. Although they are more likely at this point in their studies to encounter a more incisive and comprehensive criticism of the system than ever before, it remains occasional and fragmented and decidedly out of the mainstream in modern republican democratic higher education.

CRITIQUE OF CURRENT EDUCATIONAL PRACTICE

As far as contemporary American political science is concerned, there has been a definite increase in the degree of criticism that is tolerated in educating the future democratic elite. This criticism, begrudgingly permitted within the parameters of the continuing progressive tradition and protected through the warm embrace of the tenure system, presently incorporates those views that demonstrate the deeply embedded racist, ethnophobic, and sexist character of much of American history, and of the political economy today. A heavy component of that critique argues that the present political system is overly dominated by large, organized multinational and global economic and political organizations. This predominance leads to and justifies widescale alienation and disaffection from politics by the American citizenry. After all, if you have no say, why bother? The resulting uninvolvement thus implies approval.

On the other hand, it is fair to say that despite this new brand of systemic criticism by a small minority of American political and social scientists and historians, the prevalent sentiment remains favorable to the continuation of the system, albeit with some needed reform. These reforms, however, are marginal and combine to continue the rule of the democratic elite over the rest of the disenfranchised citizenry. There is still little information presented and little sympathy shown by the American professorate that would call for a two-way, lateral rearrangement of the power structure at the local, state, or national levels. Direct democracy, when it is mentioned at all, is critiqued more vigorously than the representative system. And the entire practice of teaching about democracy at the college and university level is about as undemocratic in pedagogy and style as that practiced in the first grade of American primary education. In some ways this criticism makes matters worse by creating a cynical, nihilistic counterelite. Pointing out the sources of political alienation without teaching how to address them merely produces a better-informed alienation and a better-rationalized hostility. Clearly, if we are to teach a constructive critique of American politics we need to do so by teaching improved democratic practice as well.

Unfortunately, the scattered elements of the modern, progressive critique have been met by a much more systematic, better-funded, and more reactionary counterattack. This well-organized and highly publicized response rejects any effort to describe the central role of higher education in reproducing gender, class, and racial divisions in society. It prefers, instead, to play down or ignore the liberal tradition's less-than-democratic tenets and to promote its own far less democratic ones. It appeals to authority grounded in classical texts that are severed from their historical eras, a disembodied humanism. In this view, the fullest expression of human potential is accommodation to the present system of social control by those without political and economic power. The practical consequence of this reactionary counterattack is to parody recent attempts within the narrow liberal tradition to expand recruitment for the next generation of political and economic elites. This counterattack brandishes as politically incorrect the political genius of that American tradition that preserves the quintessence of class structure by permitting its regular, incremental change. Those who urge a radical democratic restructuring of politics and the workplace are treated as being beneath contempt, hardly worthy of any commentary other than ridicule.

NEW PRACTICES OF DEMOCRATIC TEACHING

So what are we to do, we who are convinced that a new democratic restructuring of the educational system is necessary to germinate, stimulate, or complement a future democratic restructuring of American social, political, and economic institutions? Given the current systemic inertia, one avenue left open is that of modest experimentation at the college level. It is difficult for administrators to reject experiments in democratic teaching in the popular educational tradition, given the shields of tenure and academic freedom in American higher education. Naturally, there is precious little monetary support for such work, but little that can be done to censor or censure it either.

Popular education offers the most relevant and cogent lessons for those who would venture into democratic teaching and learning. It addresses central questions of political, social, and economic arrangements that the other traditions—technical, humanist, liberal, and progressive—ignore, take for granted, or seek merely to reform. Popular education recognizes the need to transform these elitist arrangements and respects the political impediments to doing so. Popular education broadly encompasses the education of people without ordinary access to elite-dominated educational institutions and for the purpose of social change. Ordinarily, popular education has had the goal of imparting specific skills and competencies related to concrete political objectives. The Citizenship Schools of the Highlander Folk School in the 1950s and of the Southern Christian Leadership Conference of the 1960s offer clear examples of this. Staff members of the Citizenship Schools taught literacy to African Americans in rural parts of the South so that they could acquire sufficient competency to pass literacy tests and then register to vote. During those lessons, the students discussed local needs and resources. Replicated hundreds of times, these schools became the classrooms of the civil rights movement (Glen 1988). The starting point of popular education, then, is not the grievance or deprivation of a group, but rather their desire to take action and to help develop the resources to do so.

Paulo Freire has provided the most systematically developed theory of popular education (1970, 1973; Shor and Freire 1987). The Brazilian military junta that came to power in 1964 halted Freire's adult literacy program because of its subversive premises. Freire's work prompted political opposition largely for the same reasons that authentic democratic education has risked political suppression dating back at least to the time of Socrates. First, Freire maintains that education is never politically neutral but disseminates the values of the dominant institutions and reinforces the socioeconomic distinctions within society. Therefore, for members of groups with less income and political power, education is often what he calls a "pedagogy of oppression." Second, Freire maintains that education should be empowering, and that people traditionally excluded from educational institutions should be included. The instruction they receive should serve not as socialization to dominant social and economic mores and modes but as cultural action for freedom. It should aid in the formation of critical consciousness, which is an awareness of the way dominant socioeconomic systems and processes affect people, especially the poor and the working class, in their everyday lives. Finally, education must provide the instruments to escape the doldrums and the dungeons.

Freire's linking of knowledge and action in working with poor and powerless people has led many others around the world to adopt his methods in teaching and practicing democracy. Popular education extends far beyond conventional American democratic education by teaching a central element of democracy in any setting.

For example, participatory research, one form of popular education that incorporates the principles of Freire, assumes that knowledge is related to power and that power is related to change or to maintenance of the status quo. Freire advocates the use of research to produce knowledge that will empower the powerless. One of the key assumptions of participatory research is that it will transform the very people who do the research. Advocates thus distinguish participatory research from other research, which assumes that change will come, if it comes about at all, by the action of people who read the work of others. Learning and action are thus linked and are part of a single process of democratic political change and practice.

Participatory research also assumes that ordinary people have ability as well as needs. These abilities include a clear perception of their own problems. As futurist Alvin Toffler once put it, "You don't have to be an expert to know what you want." Furthermore, most individuals have sufficient talent and intelligence to do some kind of research related to solving their problems, albeit with some expert assistance. Thus, there are several clear and distinguishing features of participatory research (Couto 1987) that are applicable to teaching democracy democratically. Numbered among them are:

- the people affected by the problem set the agenda;
- the goal is political or social change;
- the people affected by the problem control the process of problem definition, information gathering, and how to implement decisions; and

• the people affected and those who help them are equal opportunity learners in how to deal with the problem.

Participatory research, as a form of popular education, is a continuing dialogue and a mobilization of human resources for information gathering calculated to lead to action. It is a genuine Socratic dialogue because both the teacher and students engage in the questioning process that will bring answers to them both. Participatory research is also democratic because it intends to be of direct and immediate benefit to a community that controls the process from start to finish. Questions of process are decided in open discussion among everyone involved. What information do we need? How do we go about getting this information? Who is going to get the information? What does the information mean? Is it enough information? How do we interpret the information? What action seems reasonable in the light of what we have learned? How can we carry it out? How do we determine whether it is successful or not? Questions such as these imply group problem solving that is a building block of democratic action.

On the other hand, popular education offers a dilemma. It occurs outside of formal educational settings and often despite them. Thus, introducing popular education into formal, educational institutions means either transforming the purpose and practice of the schools and colleges or reforming them—in classes or courses—with insights and techniques from popular education. The latter incremental and partial alterations of institutional premises provide a starting place for later, more comprehensive changes. Successful tactics must precede any strategic gains. Democratic education will not come all at once. It can only proceed step-by-step, classroom-by-classroom, and person-by-person.

In addition to participatory research, experiential education offers another pragmatic approach to popular education. Experiential education has a well-ensconced place in American higher education. Modern American technical education depends heavily upon experiential education through internships, clinical training, apprenticeships, and other training formats. The difference, of course, is that technical training raises few questions about the democratic nature of the work or setting involved. We look in vain, for example, for the spotlight of reflection on the social correlates or ideas about the democratic reform of our health and legal systems from our medical and law schools. And it is the rare internship in criminal justice, journalism, public or business administration, and so forth, that arms its students with enough democratic theory to question the lack of democracy in any work site. Obviously, then, popular education needs more than conventional technical-experiential education. What is needed in its place is the combining of democratic theory and data with practical experience in a wide variety of settings that will provide opportunities for students to live and feel the social, economic, and political inequities that so thoroughly pervade the American institutional framework.

INSTITUTIONALIZING DEMOCRATIC EDUCATION IN AMERICA

Several prominent reports on higher education offer a starting point on the path of popular education for democratic teaching within the formal American educational system. These reports draw chiefly upon the progressive tradition and pinpoint the need to reinstate, or at least reinvigorate, democracy and civic participation into the curriculum. The heart of the problem, even from an establishment point of view, is the almost total failure of college educators "to provide for the education of citizenship" (Newman 1985:31). In addition, another authority on higher education in America concluded his survey of the undergraduate menu with "the uncomfortable feeling that the most vital issues of life—the nature of society, the roots of social injustice, indeed the very prospects for human survival—are the ones with which the undergraduate college is least equipped to deal" (Boyer 1987:283). Yet another study suggested that the actual curriculum and culture of competitiveness and individualism on most campuses undermine any prodemocratic efforts to impart values of cooperation and altruism (Astin 1987). Unsaid at this point was the uneasy but pervasive feeling that the lack of democratic virtue, altruism, and collaboration for social purposes among students indicated that students were living *down* to the expectations of the entrenched liberal tradition's "me-first," climb-the-ladder curriculum in higher education.

Other leaders in American higher education share this concern for increased democratic, socially minded education as well. In the early 1980s a set of university and college presidents, under the aegis of the Education Commission of the States, began Campus Compact, an association to encourage and support community service on campuses. In a decade, this association had attracted more than four hundred college presidents as members. Many college students also began a plethora of campus-based community service organizations, many of them linked through the Campus Outreach Opportunity League (COOL).

Then, in the spring of 1992, the staffs of the national offices of Campus Compact and COOL convened at the Highlander Research and Education Center near Knoxville, Tennessee, a hub of popular education in the United States. Highlander taught praxis—a combination of theory and practice of democracy. It preached the wisdom and virtue of education as an instrument of social and political change. After two days of discussion, participants in both Campus Compact and COOL concluded that community service had peaked in its initial phase of development. They also arrived at a mutual understanding that the next phase for community service in higher education should be integration into the curriculum, in particular through structured reflection as an integral part of a systematic learning process.

Many observers welcomed this new emphasis on reflection in community service and the move from community to curriculum and community. A leader in this type of institutionalized popular education, Harry Boyte, put it like this: "The goal of civic education should be to provide young people with hands-on public experience, with opportunities to practice political skills like strategic thinking, bargaining, negotiation, listening, argument, problem solving and evaluation" (Boyte 1991:628). However, Boyte was quick to forge the link between those skills and a theoretically grounded self-critique because, in his view, any such program should be principally "designed to move students to reflect on their lives and careers in ways that allow them to integrate their concerns with . . . the radically different interests, values, and trajectories through which people learn to engage the public world in their distinctive styles . . . [It] also draws attention to the 'commonwealth'—an exchange of reciprocal public obligations and public goods, created through common action" (Boyte 1993: 66). For this reason, Boyte prefers the concept "public service"—instead of community service—as the best way to label reflective experiential education in a broadly democratic context.

Benjamin Barber moved his discussions of "strong democracy" from the drawing board to a program of community service and reflection at Rutgers University. Barber sees education and democracy in a mutual relationship of primary interdependence. The mission of democracy is public education and the mission of education in a democracy is democracy itself. Barber also links democracy inextricably to the concept of community. Thus, to build democracy is to build community. And teaching democracy involves the teaching and practice of community building. In his words: "Civic education should be communal as well as community-based. If citizen education and experiential learning of the kind offered by community service are to be a lesson in community, the ideal learning unit is not the individual but the small team, where people work together and learn together, experiencing what it means to become a small community together" (Barber 1992: 255). We see value in both views. Experiential democratic education should involve both public and community service. It is public and communal in nature.

Both of these views, it seems to us, draw strength from the work of the preeminent democratic theorist-educator in American history, John Dewey. Boyte and Barber, like Dewey, explain that at stake is a system in which people, as citizens, learn the basic values of pure democratic citizenship, such as how to: (1) respect one another; (2) listen to one another; (3) think critically together about common problems and issues; (4) arrive at solutions to mutual problems creatively in a community setting; and (5) work together in implementing those solutions. Dewey saw the essence of democracy as "a mode of associated living, of conjoint communicated experience" (Dewey 1916: 101). Barber translates Dewey's central concern of "How can a public be organized?" into "How can a civic community [of strong democracy] be created?" (Barber 1984: 133). He explains further that experience, according to Dewey, "in its vital form is experimental, an effort to change the given; it is characterized by projection, by reading forward into the unknown; connection with a future is its salient trait" (Barber 1984: 53).

Nothing captures the essence of democratic teaching, rooted in popular education, better than the above emphasis on challenging the given nature of the present and the possibility of creating a future based on possibility rather than necessity. Freire faults most education for its failure to criticize the present and to make new futures possible. He describes ordinary teaching as banking. Teachers make deposits of information into students and at the end of the semester ask for withdrawals from students on exams and papers. Freire contrasts this style with a dynamic model that blurs distinctions of teachers and students and combines them in "an adventure of the spirit," an effort "to unveil things and facts to understand the reason for facts."

Freire finds the roots of his pedagogy in the community schools that grow from social movements and the efforts of people within those movements to acquire the education available to others and to educate themselves for political, economic, social, and personal transformation. "Liberation movements" frequently include community-based education, for example, the schools for the freed people during Reconstruction, the citizenship schools of the civil rights movement in the South, the community schools and base communities of Latin America, and the consciousness-raising groups of the women's movement.

Freire's basic question, then, one implicit in the work of Dewey and Barber, is our own central concern as well: "How is it possible to be a democratic teacher in undemocratic settings?"

DEMOCRATIC EXPERIENTIAL TEACHING IN MODERN AMERICA: HOW CAN IT WORK?

The elements of democratic experiential teaching are discernable, albeit with an emphasis on democratic theory and processes. How to make them work in the hierarchical, patriarchal, plutocratic structures of American education, government, and society is the big question. After all, the democratic teacher remains a "problem maker" who questions the value of extending the imperfect present into the future and suggests the power of humans to imagine and achieve a future more desirable than that of the present. Problem making is "trouble making," according to the elites who are working on their own future—the status quo ad infinitum. This explains why democratic teachers so often face political opposition and even repression.

However, at the American university level, the problem is more complicated than that of brute repression. Those who preach more democracy in modern-day American classrooms and who favor democratic experiential education have many other problems to solve, some of which are dilemmas wrapped in enigmas wrapped in paradoxes. They want students to practice the values of pure democracy in real life, regardless of whether it is within a government agency, the office of some political leader, or under the auspices of some established United Way organization. Obviously these places are at least in part undemocratic, if not overtly antidemocratic. How can democratic teachers deal honestly with such agencies? How can they get these agencies to evaluate the students from a democratic perspective? Can the agencies do so? Will they?

Then there are the ironies involved in the classroom itself. Democratic teachers face the real problem of dealing with the use of their own authority within elite institutions of a plutocratic system in transmitting democratic analysis and values to the student body. How can they force a democratic ideology on the students? How can they impose an evaluation system on the students? How far can professors go in allowing students sufficient independence of thought and imagination without stepping in to curtail them? So the making of problems is clearly not enough. The democratic teacher must also help to resolve them.

One way of helping students resolve these problems may be by directly transferring to them an awareness of the problems, dilemmas, and paradoxes of democratic teaching by arming them with the power and the responsibility of resolving them themselves. We have noted before that reflection must provide the cornerstone of democratic experiential education. Most experiential educators attempt to travel the cycle of learning that David Kolb has described, one in which reflection and experience support each other (see Figure I.1). Kolb's learning cycle, the Rosetta stone of experiential education, combines concrete experience through a reflective stage to a critical/analytical stage to a stage of application of new ideas which, when tested, provide concrete experience that begins the cycle again (Kolb 1984). The cycle may begin with any stage, and any learner will have many cycles going on at the same time and be at different stages in each of them. The key, however, is that the cycle of experiential education and democratic practice are lifelong and not limited to school or school-aged persons.

This shift in power and responsibility for reflecting on experience over a lifetime may be a key lesson for the bearer of the educational burden, the teacher, to learn. By diffusing power to the classroom community, that is, being truly democratic, the yoke becomes lighter and solutions more doable. By practicing what he or she preaches in the classroom, the democratic teacher may be able to best reveal the inadequately democratic nature of the

Figure I.1
Kolb's Learning Cycle

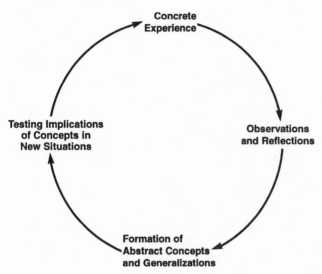

outside world in which positive, democratic experiential education and democratic transformation must take place.

THE PRACTICE OF DEMOCRATIC EXPERIENTIAL EDUCATION IN MODERN AMERICA

There have been, in recent years, several relatively successful "teaching democracy by being democratic" experiments. This book will present original essays that describe six of them, each written by an American professor who has given democratic teaching the old college try. But note that we have said "relatively" successful. What do we mean by that?

Even though all of the contributors to this book believe in the value of democratic education and have conducted what they consider to be valuable experiments in its practice, none are wild-eyed dreamers who only see the world as they think it should be. They know only too well that professors and students are not going to change the world or even that portion of it that they are using for experiential education. Any teacher who has had much experience with the democratic teaching enterprise comes to understand that the nature of the process amounts to very little in immediate transformation.

When students experience firsthand the few joys and multiple frustrations of dealing with direct democracy in a classroom or in an off-campus organizational setting, they learn a great deal about how hard it is to listen, to communicate, to deal with their feelings, to collaborate with those whom they dislike, and so forth. In addition, there is almost no outside support for what they are undertaking, yet plenty of cynicism and negative reactions, and what's more, once the experiment is completed and the student leaves it behind, it scarcely remains more than a ripple in the mainstream of their studies. They then leave the university and take their places in the hierarchical, patriarchal structures of the business or governmental real world.

When the participants look back at what was learned in the democratic classroom or in their reflective internship, will they think it was a dream world that the professor foisted upon them? Even though it worked in the university womb, how in the world can it work in "reality?" What use has it got for them now that they are on their way up the ladder to positions in which they call the shots?

It is pretty obvious to professors who have taught for a while that their impact on students, even the most idealistic and brightest among them, is usually marginal and wanes over time. And when the lesson imparted goes almost entirely against the cultural grain, the impact is even more ephemeral. The diminution effect increases geometrically in the context of the students' real-life experiences to the contrary.

No, truly democratic teachers do not do what they do because they are looking for disciples or apostles. If the aim is to change the world, the arrow will fall far from the bull's-eye. So unless the democratic teacher lives in a superutopian world or is, at heart, masochistic, other pedagogical and political goals are involved.

It seems to us that history is replete with people who have seen the struggle for human rights as something they must commit themselves to regardless of the practical obstacles and/or consequences. Some of them have given their lives to gain freedom or power for those who have been oppressed by the then-current power wielders. Many of them knew, at the moment, that prospects for success were dim, that the odds against them were astronomical. Yet they persisted in the face of repression, torture, exile, and even death. In the long run, those who paid an extreme personal price to help end slavery, to gain voting rights for women and African Americans, or other such measures were all part of movements that ultimately culminated in the triumph of their wishes for an improved American democracy.

What is the price, then, to be paid by democratic experiential teachers in modern-day America? Frustration? Marginalization? Disrespect by some peers? Parody or condemnation by those who oppose such "populism," "socialism," "radicalism?" The fact is that most of what is learned by students will be lost over time. There will be scant visible change in the system. So what *will* be gained? The life of the imagination—that is what is gained. Without imagination, neither good teaching nor democratic politics is possible. Imagination provides us the social bond to see ourselves in the conditions of others and to imagine ways in which to make conditions better for everyone.

Those American teachers who are dedicated to the view that when a democracy is ailing, what it needs most is a healthy injection of more and better democracy have little recourse in this day and age other than to retool their teaching practices. They know full well that if the end is to be more and better democracy, then the means cannot be undemocratic. But they also know that what needs to be done is to stop talking and to start teaching in an experiential, or what Dewey called experimental, mode. For what is needed is not more talk, or theory, but more experience.

As Freire wisely said, there are so many possibilities, so many paths to blaze, so many ideals to explore, so many models to fly. If nothing else, democratic teachers have little in the past to encumber their imaginations. Almost any experiment is worth trying because something worthwhile, whether positive or negative, is almost surely to be learned. As the number of these experiments increases and the lode of knowledge grows, the time may come when America is ready to learn from the pioneers in this kind of action research. Increased and improved democracy may not result from their enterprises, but it surely will not come about without them. It is that possibility, which has occurred regularly in American history, of helping some future America become more democratic, that these experiments and this book are all about.

REFERENCES

Astin, Alexander. 1987. "Competition or Cooperation." *Change* (September/October): 12-19.

Barber, Benjamin R. 1984. *Strong Democracy: Participatory Politics for a New Age.* Berkeley: University of California Press.

———. 1992. *An Aristocracy of Everyone: The Politics of Education and the Future of America.* New York: Ballantine Books.

Boyer, Ernest. 1987. *College: The Undergraduate Experience in America.* New York: Harper & Row.

Boyte, Harry C. 1991. "Turning on Youth to Politics." *The Nation* (May 13): 626-28.

———. 1993. "What is Citizenship Education?" In *Rethinking Tradition: Integrating Service with Academic Study on College Campuses,* ed. Tamar Y. Kupiec, 63–66. Providence, R.I.: Campus Compact.

Burns, James MacGregor. 1978. *Leadership.* New York: Harper & Row.

Couto, Richard A. 1987. "Participatory Research: Methodology and Critique." *The Clinical Sociology Review* 5: 83-90.

Dewey, John. 1916. *Essays in Experimental Logic.* Chicago: University of Chicago Press.

Dye, Thomas R. and Harmon Zeigler. 1996. *The Irony of Democracy.* 10th ed. Belmont, Calif.: Wadsworth Publishing Co.

Freire, Paulo. 1970. *Pedagogy of the Oppressed*. New York: Continuum Publishing Co.

———. 1973. *Education for Critical Consciousness*. New York: Continuum Publishing Co.

Glen, John. 1988. *Highlander: No Ordinary School, 1932–1962*. Lexington: University Press of Kentucky.

Johansen, Bruce E. 1982. *The Forgotten Founders: How the American Indian Helped Shape Democracy*. Boston: Harvard Common Press.

Kolb, David A. 1984. *Experiential Learning: Experience as the Source of Learning and Development*. Englewood Cliffs, N.J.: Prentice-Hall.

Newman, Frank. 1985. *Higher Education and the American Resurgence*. Princeton, N.J.: Carnegie Foundation for the Advancement of Teaching.

Parenti, Michael. 1983. *Democracy for the Few*. 4th ed. New York: St. Martin's Press.

Rousseau, Jean-Jacques. 1950. *The Social Contract*. 1762; New York: Dutton.

Shor, Ira and Paulo Freire. 1987. *A Pedagogy for Liberation: Dialogues on Transforming Education*. New York: Bergin & Garvey.

PART I

The Democratic Classroom

In the early 1970s, there were two extremely different kinds of experiments in democratic classrooms being conducted in two vastly different worlds. In Communist China, under the aegis of Maoist theory, a great leveling was underway in a movement that worshipped equality. In this view of democracy, it was all-important that there be no ranking of individuals. Everyone was equal in status. The officer corps in the army was abolished and there were simply soldiers—no generals, no privates. Intellectuals were compelled to spend part of their lives harvesting crops, making them one with the peasantry.

In the schools of the cultural revolution, equality was the rule, no exceptions. No one was allowed to be dressed better than anyone else. Thus, all schoolchildren wore the same kind of clothes. Furthermore, they could not compete with one another or try to excel at the expense of anyone else. In this view of democracy, students had to learn to colabor for the maximum benefit of society. In fact, the buttons on their uniforms were placed in the back so that no student could dress or undress without the help of another. Cooperation was paramount—for the greater glory of China.

In capitalist America, another "democratic revolution" was also brewing. It was a time of great foment and turbulence in the colleges and universities, where students railed against the system and demanded "power to the people." There were sit-ins in administrative offices, with groups of students seek-

/58,407

LIBRARY
College of St. Francis
JOLIET, ILLINOIS

ing entry into the decision-making process of higher education. They wanted—no, demanded—influence in university
budget making, foreign investments and, most important, in
the content of the curriculum and in the grading system.

So, in many American universities, a large number of experiments in student participation in the curriculum and in the
evaluation process were devised and carried out. The University of Hawaii, for instance, established "New College" for students who wanted to design and carry out their own learning
experience in higher education.

The Maoist educational experiment, in pursuit of the so-
called "people's democracy," eventually failed as Maoism fell
into some disrepute and much disrepair. Individualism, competition, and capitalism have made a major comeback on
mainland China and status is again prized by many Chinese
and endorsed by the ruling Communist Party.

In the United States the democratic classrooms and colleges, including Hawaii's "New College," were short lived. Students who were left to their own devices floundered. The lack
of knowledge-based, teacher-inspired curriculum led to intellectual chaos. The result was a mountain of negative feeling
and a molehill of positive learning.

Thus, it should be quite clear that trying to democratize
classrooms is not easy. There is great potential for failure.
There exists a paradox that, if not fully understood by all concerned, will probably be fatal. A practical democratic structure
must be created by careful planning and mutual agreement
between the teacher and the students. The tone of the classroom must be one of tentative truth-through-experimentation,
not orthodox truth-via-dogma.

The overwhelming preponderance of teachers in all societies are not the least bit interested in teaching democracy by
being democratic. Those who are interested must engage in
an extremely time-consuming, energy-sapping experience. It
is not surprising, therefore, that there is not a surfeit of actual
democratic classroom experimentation.

What follows are two accounts written by teachers so committed to the empowering aspect of authentic democracy that
they incorporated its principles into the organization of their
own classrooms. What they discovered was that they, like
their students, had a lot to learn.

Students in Charge

William R. Caspary

There are many ways to structure democratic classrooms, such as combinations of small-group and large-group activity, in-class and outside-class activities, distribution of facilitation tasks and presentation tasks, and so on. In my own classes, an independent inquiry project outside of the classroom—pursued singly or in groups—has been a key element. Class time is divided between small-group and whole-group discussion, facilitated by the students themselves. These innovations are usually phased in gradually. Once the transition is made, my role is that of a participant with no special privileges, though one with more experience and information. On occasion, at the students' request or even on my suggestion, I will give a minilecture to provide background on some topic. In this brief chapter the focus will not only be on structure and process, as important as those topics may be, but on underlying rationales as well.

CLASSROOMS AS IF STUDENTS MATTERED

I went to the circus recently and watched the acrobats do high-wire acts without a net. It reminded me of when I first experimented with democratic classrooms. Scary, but exhilarating! Those classes involved giving up the security, the safety net, of professorial authority backed by the power of grades. The security of familiar routines and well-honed academic skills had to be yielded as well. Instead, there was on-the-spot improvisation to solve problems I hadn't encountered before—and falling on my face if it didn't work out. In writing this chapter I hope I can make it a bit easier for others to try these experiments, or at least to assure them that the blunders and pitfalls are not all that painful, while the results will be well worth the effort.

As for the students in these classes, given their background of conventional schooling, they were as unprepared for the democratic classroom as I was. Self-initiated and self-directed learning was something of which they could scarcely conceive, much less carry out. In their prior schooling experience they had learned to be combative toward and distrustful of each other, which made cooperative learning a new and difficult, if not impossible task. As I witnessed the students struggling to collaborate, the task of building cooperative environments and skills seemed all the more urgent. It was only by trying something new that I realized fully how bad the old system was. It was only by letting go of the crutches of authoritarian classrooms that we discovered how crippled we had become in relying on them.

This discovery in itself meant that from the very outset the experiment was teaching us all something. Even as we struggled to fulfill other goals, we were already succeeding in the goal of becoming awakened, acute observers of conventional structures of everyday life and their effects upon us. Also, the sheer fact that we were doing something different was a revelation. We had come to believe that everything was as it must be, that, even though discontented, we were powerless to make any changes. Students were also amazed that I would respect and trust them enough to involve them in the management of the course. This suggested how little they'd felt respected and trusted before. Formerly, I had thought myself a rather benevolent despot, dispensing wisdom and caring for each of my students as individuals. And the teacher ratings had been good. So it was a bit of a shock to discover that only the renunciation of that authority succeeded in fully communicating respect and trust.

I'll make a brief statement at the outset of my basic value commitments and understandings of democracy, which I hope will provide orientation to the discussion that follows. I'm committed to John Dewey's view that "democracy is a way of personal life controlled . . . by faith in the capacity of human beings for intelligent judgment and action if proper conditions are furnished . . . faith in personal day to day working together with others" (Dewey 1939:241-42). This is consistent with Paulo Freire's ideas about dialogical, problem-posing education, in which professors become teacher-learners and students become learner-teachers. It also fits his understanding of education as an arena for a democratic practice which, within the classroom, overcomes hierarchy and oppression. I weave this together with Immanuel Kant's dictum that each person is an end, not a means, and with Mahatma Gandhi's nonviolent philosophy of love for each person—even one's adversaries. Finally, the method of active listening, derived from the work of Carl Rogers on empathy, provides a practical working out of these ideals.

These concerns for the interpersonal aspects of democracy do not mean a lack of concern for the macroscopic problems of democratic processes in complex societies. A Gandhian concern for nonviolence does not imply any lack of awareness of power, privilege, and oppression. I do not overlook the capitalist economic system and its putative contributions to inequality in access and influence in political life. Nonetheless, in the struggle for equality and justice, in political discourse, in the inner life of social movements, I see the interpersonal aspect of democracy as crucial. The values of mutuality, dialogue, and nonviolence can be seen as indispensable microfoundations for democracy in larger spheres.

These understandings of democracy demand a great deal of individual citizens, teachers, and students. I believe, however, that anything less than this would be insufficient. The pathologies of our present imperfect democracy and the inability of social movements to overcome them, in my view, are traceable, in part, to the failure to recognize, propagate, and live by these values. The task is not to develop some easier compromise version, but to discover and implement the transformational programs through which these high ideals can be realized. The classroom, then, becomes a laboratory for inquiry into this vital project.

Personally speaking, I know that I cannot fully achieve these values in my own life and teaching, but I can strive toward realizing them and grow in my capacity to fulfill them. This growth comes both from working toward self-awareness and integration in my private life and from learning directly from experience in the classroom. To illustrate this theme of growth in the teacher, I'll mention a particular issue. Approaching democracy on the interpersonal level suggests a more personal relationship with students than the conventional one permits. It requires, therefore, an increased understanding of and respect for boundaries. Concern for the humanness of students is not an excuse for intruding upon their privacy and autonomy; indeed it precludes such invasiveness. Nor is the imposition upon the students of my own private concerns, troubles, and needs consistent with respect for their personhood (Miller 1981). The term intrusiveness certainly covers the issue of sexual harassment, which is so prominent at this time, but it also involves a much broader range of intellectual and emotional issues. This understanding of boundaries requires that I work on improving my private life—both my self-awareness and my ability to meet my needs—so that I don't unknowingly act out personal issues in the classroom.

With these thoughts as prologue, I'll proceed to a detailed discussion of pedagogical and theoretical issues in the democratic classroom as I've experienced them.

SELF-INITIATED AND SELF-DIRECTED LEARNING: THE TERM PROJECT

One of the most important products of the course is a term project to be carried out using democratic self-initiating methods. This challenge elicits anxiety in the students and poses a host of pedagogical problems for the professor. The following discussion will spell out the sorts of projects that are undertaken and reflect on the practical and theoretical issues that arise.

1. The students are asked to generate their own questions, hypotheses, or theories about democracy and then to organize and motivate their work around them. Some students, for example, are appalled at what they see as the superficiality, sensationalism, and bias in contemporary news reporting. Several of them, therefore, have devoted their projects to research that identifies the social forces that prevent higher quality journalism and how these might be overcome. Other students may have been concerned about excessive government bureaucracy and believe that market forces are a much better mechanism for making social choices. Some students are more disposed to seeking out a field experience, conducting participant-observer research. Others are concerned with the politics of identity in contemporary democratic life. Still others are intrigued by democratic education itself as it might be developed in the school system and at the college level. All of these concerns point to fairly specific topics within which a particular project can be developed.

The possibilities are manifold, and there will always be wonderful questions and approaches arising from students' particular experiences and viewpoints that I could never anticipate. Where students already have such ideas in mind or can arrive at them fairly quickly, my principle task is to encourage them, offer resources and suggestions, and make it clear that originality and risk taking will not be punished. I also take it as my job to nudge students to get started quickly so they have time to do justice to the project and to finish in time to share their work with the class. Since many of these projects will be narrowly focused, the hope for broad understanding of democratic theory will lie in the exchange of ideas among the students and in common readings and class discussions.

2. A substantial number of students, however, have no such topics in mind. Many students in the past have told me that they had absolutely no experience in forming and pursuing their own inquires. They had not the vaguest notion where to begin and this left them acutely uncomfortable. What an indictment of our educational system! It is only when I stopped assigning typical term papers on a range of prescribed topics that I discovered how incapacitated students had become in initiating and directing their own learning. Often students insisted that I tell them what I wanted them to work on or manipulated me subtly to reveal my hidden agenda for them. There was a temptation on my part to escape the discomfort that we all were feeling by giving the students a project. But that would have been cheating the students.

I try instead to respond with cues and methods for brainstorming, exploring, and reflecting. I try to relieve the pressure to come up with ideas immediately by suggesting that discovering these learning goals is a process that takes time over the course of learning, not something one does prior to starting out. I also encourage students not to get locked into the first project that they start upon, but to feel free to let their goals evolve and change. This past semester there were enough students who had difficulty formulating objectives that I returned to a procedure I worked out years ago: a series of pencil-and-paper exercises and small group discussion exercises for eliciting questions, interests, and concerns, and then refining these into educational objectives. This proved useful for developing the agenda for class discussion, as well as for individual projects. Unfortunately, we arrived at this solution late in the semester. It will be introduced early next time. In my experience, the democratic classroom is experimental, a never-ending learning process.

Listening to other students' questions, concerns, and objectives during class discussion and small-group exercises evokes ideas about objectives in those students who lack them. Our conventional system tends to isolate students and deprive them of this dynamic interaction. Intellectual community is crucial for democratic education. My goal is the creation of a stimulating, supportive climate of interchange, not one of students learning in a vacuum, or learning in competition with one another, or in a one-on-one relationship with the teacher.

3. Student biases and blind spots give rise to another key pedagogical issue. Suppose self-directed learning is taken as an opportunity to organize one's project around a biased view and is designed in such a way as to protect that prejudice from any challenge? In traditional education there is a demand that the student be objective and rational—that any position be defended with valid evidence and argument. In practice, however, this often forces prejudices underground and develops a split between private belief and public academic performance. In proposing an alternative, I will first state a broad theoretical and value orientation and then discuss pedagogical practices.

The concept of the class as a learning community is a key part of the answer to this problem, as it was to the previous one. In a well-functioning community, the encounter with and respect for the views of others is a natural and powerful counterweight to a particular student's bias. A student's peers can often be more influential than a professor, to whom a student may feel compelled to defer publicly and, in reaction, to resist stubbornly in her or his private thought.

People are not fixed, static entities. The Rogerian and Deweyan view, which I am persuaded is accurate, is that who we are and what we believe are always in process. As a teacher, I wish to help students move forward in their own processes, not mine. I trust that, on the whole, this process moves in positive directions—even if I can't see at this moment how that will come about, or even if the direction at this moment is one that seems negative to me. I think far more damage is done in our schools and in our society by our distrust of and interference with the individual inclinations of our students.

However, there is a view among some theorists that is quite opposite to mine. What is at stake, in their view, is not an individual's *process* of learning and development, but an individual who has already been shaped by societal forces. This shaping inevitably reflects the ideologies that defend existing institutions and distributions of privilege. The professor, therefore, must use his or her position of authority to exert a counterforce to reform the student in the direction of critical and emancipatory ideals. Though plausible and tempting on its surface, I think this view is, at bottom, profoundly antidemocratic. I shall discuss this key issue at greater length below. For the moment, let me note that the very fact of my renunciation of my position of formal authority may communicate more and better information of reformative value than any ideas that I could convey by employing its leverage to purge students of harmful ideologies.

As a teacher, then, I need to walk the tightrope between encouraging students to move comfortably in their chosen directions and revealing my discomfort with their enterprises. I need to support them in the free exploration of their own questions and intuitions and at the same time express my honest disagreement, or even dismay, and to *suggest* (not recommend) other views and approaches. The more the students can let go of the image of me as a controlling authority, the more I am free to express my views openly.

I recall a research project a student did some years ago on the theoretical issue of negative freedom and positive freedom. The work was motivated by his deep-seated and passionately held laissez faire, conservative ideology. Despite intense, albeit respectful, exchanges with his classmates, his views were unwavering. I took up my own role as a commentator on his written work. The student was constantly tempted to misrepresent—as I saw it— the literature on positive freedom so as to make a stronger case for negative freedom. It was relatively easy to point to the specific texts and question his interpretation. It was also possible to refer him to communitarian critiques of the negative freedom position. But it was important to respect his deep, personal dispositions and commitments; to listen intently to his presentation of them; to see what I might learn from his views and how my views might be changed; and to encourage him to plumb his intuitions as deeply as possible. If I wished to teach him to respect positions other than his own, the most effective way to do so was to respect his.

4. In discussing self-initiated learning, I often find myself talking about how the conventional model of the term paper has shaped and limited students' ideas of learning. At best a term paper can be highly self-initiated, full of discovery, and can teach the valuable lesson of carrying a project through to closure. The actuality, however, usually falls far short of this ideal.

The conventional term paper is an adaptation to severe time constraints, to grade pressures, and to the artificial division of learning into departments, subfields, and topics within those fields. Because of these constraints, one has to pick one's topic ahead of time rather than let it emerge from exploration. One must limit the scope of one's inquiry to what is manageable in an abbreviated time and space. There's a premium on knowing where the inquiry will go before one undertakes it—outlining the paper and using one's reading to fill in the predetermined slots. It's like "cooking" a lab experiment—writing the report before one goes into the lab and filling in the blanks from the measurements one makes or even forcing the measurements to yield predetermined figures—a procedure that utterly defeats the spirit of experimental science.

If the term paper research opens up new questions and/or reveals that the original question has obvious or trivial answers, the student is pressured to suppress the exciting new issues, often slogging ahead on a project that has lost its vitality. There are times, of course, when the struggle to finish a task—to keep faith with one's commitment to a project—is very valuable. I don't want to appear to honor work that lacks commitment and effort and that strives toward closure—I take those values seriously in my own work and hope that it communicates them. But closure for its own sake, or for the grade's sake, ends up suppressing inquiry, chilling curiosity, and teaching the lesson that academic work is drudgery.

Given the prevailing emphasis on finishing a project at any cost, I tend to encourage students to engage in a much more open-ended, adventurous, and significant sort of inquiry—the kind in which a genuinely creative scholar engages (when the pressure of publish or perish doesn't force that person into the same sort of formulaic activity as the college term paper). This more open-ended approach raises anxieties in me as well as in the students. All of my training conditions me to look for a concrete, finished and polished piece of work at the end of the course—something to hold on to, some tangible evidence of my success as a teacher as well as theirs as students. I do my best to overcome my own professional training. I try to keep in mind that we, as well as our understandings, are always developing and that any product of our work is a step in this process, not a finality.

5. The range of questions, topics, and goals will probably be wide, and the individual projects rather specialized. Thus, there is a danger of centrifugal forces pulling the class away from any common enterprise and narrowing the perspectives of the individuals. This tendency toward diffusion has been especially pronounced in my present class with unfortunate results. The solution I plan to attempt next is to work more, sooner, and more explicitly to build a common class discussion agenda and to develop individual objectives within that framework. At best this will achieve more mutuality of purpose by opening up fresh possibilities, but there is always the risk of

achieving commonality by seeming to discourage divergent interests—another case of walking a tightrope.

Whatever the topics chosen, there are opportunities for integration of the material, and of the community, if the individual efforts can be shared in class discussion—shared while in progress as well as upon completion. If this is to occur, the students will need to work out the mechanisms for such sharing—formally and informally and inside and outside of class.

PROBLEMS IN EVALUATION AND GRADING

The question of evaluation and grades inevitably comes up. My current approach is that this is a matter to be decided by the class. Unless they can fully and freely decide on this issue, the shadow of the professor's power to grade will hang over everything and have the potential to pervert the entire experiment. Past classes have handled this issue responsibly, and the department and the university in which I work have not intervened to forbid this practice. Other professors in other institutions may not find that they have this leeway. That having been said, I can offer my own views on evaluation and grades for what they are worth. I've striven to step outside of the conventional institutional and theoretical frameworks that usually constrain the discussion of this topic. I hope, therefore, that I have something novel to add to an otherwise belabored and hackneyed discourse.

Let me separate evaluation from grades and talk first about the former at length. Part of empowerment for democratic citizenship is moving toward self-evaluation and away from dependence on the evaluation of others, particularly that of authority figures. This means not just internalizing the evaluations and standards of others, but also finding the standards that arise from our own deeply held and personal values, aspirations, cultural and subcultural identities, and life experiences. It means opening up such standards, once discovered, to dialogue with others, to development, experimentation, criticism, and change. The process of discovering and learning to trust our own standards, even when they are at odds with the ones prevailing in society, can be exhilarating and liberating, but sometimes difficult and gradual as well, fraught with doubt and anxiety.

We may be tempted to think of such standards as fixed, like compass points—whether these are determined by some external universal value or by some fixed essence within ourselves. But, in practice, our standards grow and change as we do, hopefully becoming richer as our understandings deepen. Our standards, like ourselves, are always in process. Each completed task is also a step in a chain of activities, as Dewey emphasizes, a part of some larger project. Therefore, we can't know the full meaning of an activity, or learning, or accomplishment until much later. So any evaluation at the time is partial and intrinsically inaccurate. We have to take it with a grain of salt and put some faith in the process.

Our standards can be too low, permitting slackness; but they can also be too high, making unrealistic demands upon ourselves. Our criteria and assessments can oppress us as well as guide us. This situation varies from person to person, but on the whole it seems that American society encourages an obsessive and debilitating preoccupation with evaluation and self-evaluation. (One can see this in popular magazines offering self-assessment tests along with articles about how to improve our ratings. Why so little self-acceptance? What does this say about our society and economy—about democracy as it is practiced and as it might be practiced?) There should be more time, in my view, to just do and just be, without a part of ourselves standing to the side watching and judging. It is an interesting paradox that when we worry less about evaluation we often achieve more.

One way to escape the oppression of evaluation is to see that it is relative to the task, the context, and the stage of our development. A successful performance in the college drama workshop is a hit, even if it would not play on Broadway. An expression of belief may be of great value when printed on the opinion page of a newspaper, even though a scholarly journal wouldn't consider it. These are two different contexts, two different functions, each with their own distinct standards, neither being intrinsically better.

Evaluation is most useful when it is prospective, not retrospective—when it suggests what I can improve in the future, rather than how I ought to feel about what I did in the past. Evaluation is most useful if it is specific rather than global, and contingent and personal rather than absolute. For example: "I don't understand how this conclusion follows from that premise; please explain," is more useful than the cryptic red penciled note: "Faulty logic!" Self-evaluations can use input from others, but they leave oneself as the final arbiter. Input from other people is often more useful to us if it is acknowledged that it comes from their own point of view—not some universal objective view to which they have privileged access. These ideas about evaluation go back to works written many decades ago by Carl Rogers, Paulo Freire, John Dewey, Erich Fromm, and others. But they also match up closely with contemporary ideas on the nature of knowledge and value—ideas that go by the labels *thick description, contextuality, situatedness, pluralism,* and so on.

Let us now consider how far college grading is from the model of self-evaluation that has just been offered. Grades come from the other, not the self. Students often say that they have not the faintest idea of "how they did" until they see the grade. Grades are global, not contextual. They take little account of process, but look at a particular fixed product. Yet they cast their shadow upon the whole process and upon the person. Too often, whether the professor intends it or not, whether we "know better" or not, a low grade is felt as diminishing to one as a person. It is a wound to our sense of worth. Because the grade is not an evaluation for use in a particular context, and because it sums up multiple dimensions in a single figure, its standards are fuzzy. There is a substantial risk of arbitrariness and injustice.

One natural response to the imprecision of grades is to try to make the standards increasingly explicit and the measurements by these standards increasingly precise and objective. But every gain we make in precision involves a trade-off in validity. The task—paper, or exam, or short-answer test— ceases to represent the sort of complex understandings and skills we are seeking to teach. The grade becomes a more and more accurate measure of less and less. Worse than misrepresenting the student's actual attainment, the grade begins to subvert attainment as the student studies only to beat the test. What was intended as the criterion of the task ends up becoming the task itself.

We live in an imperfect world, yet much that is positive goes on within it. Many students learn a great deal despite these conditions, also learning to navigate among the shoals without capsizing. But the damage done to many other students also exists, and I have begun to think that it is immense. In some previous experimental courses, I have invited students to devise their own answers to the problem of grades. Their discussions have revealed how battered some students feel by the grading system; how capricious and cruel it feels to them; how it has depressed their desire to learn and thwarted their impulses toward solidarity and cooperation with their classmates. Other students, who feel that they personally can shrug off the grades and go their own way, sympathized with the first group and agreed with their view that the system is unjust and misguided. To be sure, there are also students who see no problem with the system and their views must be respected. But some from among this group have reconsidered their position in the course of our discussions.

In several previous classes, students were provoked by our discussions to question the entire university policy. They decided, without any prompting from me, to conduct informal surveys on other professors' and students' views of the grading system. The prevailing reaction was one of deep discontent with the system, accompanied by the conviction that there is no alternative. Professors, who might have been expected to defend their own practices, expressed distress at the inaccuracy and unfairness of the present system. Some brought up the effect of grades in depressing learning and the barriers they set up between student and student, and student and professor. On the other hand, professors felt grading was necessary for two reasons: (1) students wouldn't do the work if there wasn't the threat of the grade to compel them, and (2) grades are needed so employers and graduate schools can select a small number of people out of many applicants for highly desirable positions. The students surveyed also pointed to these two rationales.

My own view is that the first problem—getting students to do the work— is an artifact of the system we have set up. We thwart students' natural curiosity and intrinsic motivation, failing to build a lively intellectual community. Thus, there's nothing left to do but to force students to work. I call this the "maraschino cherry" approach to education: To make a maraschino cherry you first bleach out all the natural color. Then you pump in a red dye. After I first formulated this view, it turned out that red dye # 2, the artificial color then in use, was poisonous!

Students' actual response to freedom from grade pressure, as I've observed it, has varied widely. At any time there will be some students who, though well intentioned, are so alienated by previous schooling experience that finding intrinsic motivation will be extremely difficult for them. In the 1960s, the mood of rebelliousness led many students into a defiant rejection of all academic work. During the 1980s, on the other hand, the students' habitual striving and dutifulness carried over to our democratic class. However, after one particular course featuring self-grading continued for a number of years, it gained a reputation and attracted freeloaders. This spoiled the experience for everyone, so I stopped teaching that course for a time. Most students are not at either extreme of the spectrum. Their response has depended to a considerable extent on whether a strong sense of community was achieved in the class and whether a bond was formed with me as a mentor. On the whole, the academic quality of the work has been on a par with what I've received in conventional classes—no miracles, no debacles. The difference has been that many projects have been more creative and more personally meaningful than those in regular courses. One indication of that result has been in my experience while reading student project reports, which has gone from being a chore to being a pleasure. Each project is unique and the individuality of the students reveals itself. No more wading through assembly line products. No more agonized wondering if the students really learned anything at all—except how to talk the jargon and beat the test.

There are several sources of motivation that replace grade pressures. The central intrinsic motivation for learning is wanting to make sense of the world one lives in and of oneself living in it. An additional fundamental motivation is the pleasure of exercising one's capabilities—exercising in both senses: activity and improvement. And there is the adventure and discovery that goes with meaningful inquiry. If we are skeptical about the existence or power of such motivations, I suggest it is because our system has done so much to suppress them, not because they are not native to all human beings.

There is yet another set of motivations that come from a learning community. For many of the students, there develops a sense of ownership of and pride in the class. Hence a wish to contribute to its success evolves, along with a desire not to let one's fellow students down. This community can provide intellectual stimulation as well as evoking loyalty. In a class characterized by a lot of interaction, the students invite, encourage, and provoke one another to raise questions and to explore new topics. In some classes there will be efforts at inclusion toward students who seem reluctant to be involved and/or social pressures toward people who are not perceived to be contributing their share.

One of the chief barriers to learning is not so much lack of motivation as fear of failure! In a student-directed classroom, some of the success-failure mentality associated with grade pressures can be eliminated at the outset. But we also find the need to help each other work through the lingering effect of those pressures as we have internalized them over many years of grade-driven education. There are also anxieties about doing open-ended exploratory work when one has been habituated to rule following. Finally, and perhaps most interesting, there are anxieties about exploring material that threatens cherished hopes or beliefs. A student-directed course can do much to provide mutual support when students risk facing such intellectual and emotional challenges. Discovering these deeply rooted and group-based motivations and supports tells us something about ourselves, about human nature, about group dynamics, and not least, about democracy. Of course there will be some students who, out of rebellion, or cynicism, or simply due to pressure from other courses, exploit this freedom to evade work. But every professor knows that some students are quite expert at beating the system of grade pressures too.

The second problem—the grade-point-average (GPA) as the ticket to future job and education opportunities—is a more genuine one. Hopefully before we work out some practical response to it, we can use it as an occasion for critique. Why are good jobs and good educational opportunities so scarce? Why can't every competent person who wants to serve in a responsible position in the field of health care, for example, find a niche for such service? Why do we drastically limit access to such positions, overload the aspirants with stress and competition, and then pay outsized salaries to compensate for all that punishment—while vast numbers of people in rural areas and inner cities are scarcely served at all? What kind of a social structure and economic system is it that creates this scarcity, and what other sorts of systems might we envision? Is such scarcity compatible with democracy?

When the students in my previous democratic classrooms proceeded to make suggestions for a new approach to grading, many options were offered. Proposals included: self-evaluation, group evaluation, dialogue between teacher and student, a single class grade, pass/fail for everyone, and various combinations of these. They also included evaluations based on process or product, effort or outcome, and so on. In practice, my classes have tried all of these methods at different times. All of them have advantages and disadvantages.

Perhaps the best experience came when we succeeded in getting the pa-

pers done and reproduced in time so students could give each other feedback. In anticipation of such feedback, one student said, "I'm going to have
to work really hard on this paper. I can bullshit the professor but I can't
get away with that with my fellow students." But giving feedback was not
giving grades. We felt it would be unfair to burden students with the responsibility of grading one another. So we still had to find a mechanism for
getting marks into the book. Our preference was for no grades at all, but
this was not an option we were free to pursue. The means of assigning the
grades was an expedient for satisfying the external demands. We did not fall
into the rationalization that the particular method we chose was something
valuable in itself.

In these deliberations on grading, consensus was extremely difficult to
reach. We realized that any option we chose would end up being unfair to
some of the students in the class. Or, if we treated ourselves with extra
latitude, we'd end up being unfair to others outside the class whose tran-
scripts would someday be compared with those of our students. Despite the
lack of fully satisfactory solutions we have, nonetheless, in the process of
struggling toward them, learned about ourselves and our society. We've
learned about communication and conflict resolution, and we've examined
our society with its hierarchies and "meritocracies," its scarcity of good jobs
and learning opportunities, its grading and stamping of human beings as if
they were machines or sides of beef.

ANOTHER CASE OF STANDARDS: EVALUATING
ARTICLES SUBMITTED TO SCHOLARLY JOURNALS

Before leaving the subject of evaluation let me add some further experiences and reflections, based on my experience as a reviewer of manuscripts
for professional journals, an arena in which problems of evaluation are considerably more straightforward and tractable than grading in college. These
journals are places for finished, polished work that has something new to
say and meets high standards of logical argumentation, valid methodology,
and theoretical insight. The journal doesn't ask me to judge the work as
good or bad, or to give it a letter grade, or to make judgments about the
intelligence, character, or future prospects of the author. Instead I'm asked
whether this article, in its present form, is suitable for this particular publication and whether I can envision the sorts of revisions that would make it
acceptable.

This is a system characterized by at least a semblance of justice. If the
results are sometimes experienced by the author as harsh, they are nonetheless presumably fair and in the service of truth. Lest there be any doubt
about my concern for standards, given my questioning of grades and advocacy of student self-evaluation, I should report that in many years of re-

viewing I have rarely recommended a paper for acceptance, even with revisions. The best evaluation I've been able to reach, with rare exceptions, is "revise and resubmit," and I've often felt the only professional conclusion is outright rejection. My sense is that I'm not being inappropriately harsh, but implementing an ideal of scholarship.

If only evaluation of term papers in college courses were as unambiguous and as circumscribed as reviewing articles for journals seems to be! But even the case of evaluations for journals is fraught with difficulties—difficulties that were deliberately omitted in the oversimplified picture that I just sketched. In fact, even standards for finished scholarly work are full of complexities and ambiguities. By way of example, an article submitted to three readers frequently receives the most disparate responses imaginable. It will be accepted without revision and, indeed, with high praise by reviewer #1, judged as needing substantial revisions by reviewer #2, and considered unacceptable, even if thoroughly revised, by reviewer #3. This is not to say that there are no standards, that anything goes, or that the reviewers are necessarily irresponsible and self-serving, but rather that standards provide broad guidelines and require subjective interpretation in order to apply them. It is to say that judgments about method and judgments about content are not so easily separated as it would appear and that substantive concerns and methodological standards are evolving, not fixed. Our reviews, then, are part of ongoing conversation and conflict within a scholarly community about our values, not precise logical inferences from fixed rules (see Kuhn 1977).

To be candid, sometimes reviewers employ the inherent ambiguity of the standards to intrude their professional, personal, or political biases. As a result, some authors are denied a forum for worthwhile work and their careers are delayed or damaged. And since it is not as easy in practice as it is in principle to separate the person from the product, unfavorable reviews can be shattering to the confidence of a scholar—especially the contemptuous reviews that occur too frequently. Destructive self-questioning and paralysis of productivity can result. Or, equally destructive, the scholar's work may be tailored to suit prevailing fashions and may be published only after altering or hiding what is original—just those things that would make a genuine contribution to the advancement of knowledge.

Knowing this, some scholars become engaged in the politics of our profession, seeking positions on editorial boards and funding agencies. Then their group can be the one to impose its values through the review process. Individually, meanwhile, some of us make the best of an imperfect situation, trying to do our reviewing responsibly. We try to be candid with ourselves and the author when our evaluations reflect our own particular perspective, not some universal Olympian view. Honesty about this imperfect intellectual/political reality is quite chastening with regard to our pretensions of lofty impartiality and adherence to precise impersonal standards.

COMMUNITY AND CONFLICT IN DEMOCRATIC CLASSROOMS

There is a substantial disparity from student to student in the degree to which they are able to initiate their own intellectual enterprises and in the level of skills that they bring to the task. What is more, there may be serious difficulties in finding a common language and some common purposes among them. This may be compounded by emotional expressions of impatience and irritation, envy and resentment. There is a strong tendency, particularly among young people, to exhibit surface brusqueness and seeming arrogance to cover up underlying insecurities. In my classes in recent years, such negative communication has increasingly appeared and has been a major obstacle to community building in the classroom.

This negative communication was particularly true of a course I offered in the spring of 1994. Seeing the class mired in a myriad of unresolved conflicts and rampant distrust, I finally proposed that the students get some systematic training in communication skills over a two-week period. I've been doing such training workshops for school teachers and community groups over many years and I offered this to the class. The students accepted and were very quick in learning the skills—one of the most able groups I've ever worked with. A week after the training was completed, one student, using the skills and her own warmth and tact, confronted the deepest underlying conflict in the class. With her leadership, the other students' active participation, and some facilitation on my part, the conflict was resolved to a considerable extent. The student who took the leadership role told me later that through the role playing exercises during the training period she had come to know some of the individuals involved in the conflict in a whole new way. Thus, those exercises had facilitated direct communication, as well as providing skills for later use. I can't say every party to the conflict was satisfied with the outcome because I haven't spoken with all of them, but the class atmosphere did change dramatically. There was a new spirit of trust and a sense of belonging and loyalty. People were much more revealing of their ideas and of themselves. The last three weeks of the semester, devoted to presentations and class discussion of student projects, were highly productive and satisfying.

A similar impasse arose in my fall 1994 class. Again I proposed communication skills and conflict resolution training. Again the class atmosphere improved substantially as a result. In this case, it seemed that there was no single focal conflict, but rather a diffuse tension over different temperamental styles of communication and learning, different levels of commitment, differing preferences for more organized or more spontaneous organizational process, and perhaps unspoken ideological differences. It appeared that after the communication training, students were more aware of and tolerant of differing styles and more willing to listen supportively to one another's views.

Given this experience, I will, from now on, introduce the communication skills package as an early, regular feature in my democratic classroom. More and more, I believe that communication skills, conflict resolution, and mediation are essential to classrooms, communities, and democratic society as a whole. It seems to me that the typical American's response to conflict is denial, avoidance, exit, domination, appeal to someone in a power position, or escalation and violence. What is it about our social and economic system that has generated these destructive behaviors and failed to provide positive alternatives? In a complex society conflict is inevitable, but it can be a source of positive change. If we wish to increase democracy we must find and disseminate new skills and values that enable us to engage in conflict productively. The very scarcity of such positive models presents great opportunity for significant social change if transformational approaches to communication and conflict can be widely propagated.

There is a risk, however, in presenting communication skills at the outset of the class. Without a perceived need arising out of class experiences and struggles, the students may not be as motivated and the training may not be as effective; so my next attempt to present this material will really be further experimentation and experiential learning. It is my hope that, when students develop more understanding of and respect for one another, we can all become, in Freire's terms, teacher-learners and learner-teachers. To the extent that we have succeeded in that endeavor, we have modeled ways in which society as a whole can cope with problems of diversity and turn them into community-building options.

RESOLVING STUDENT PROBLEMS WITH A LOSS OF TRADITIONAL AUTHORITY

There is considerable resistance on the part of some students to surrender the traditional mode just because it is familiar, whether or not they find it gratifying. The ideas of self-starting, self-direction, and self-evaluation seem bewildering and menacing to some, if not to many. Other students see them as more demanding than their usual response of just getting by in a course with precisely spelled-out requirements. Some students feel that cherished values and beliefs will be threatened. The threats may emanate from other students as they argue points during discussions or from professors as, under the cloak of professionalism or impartiality, they pursue their own agendas. The sort of inquiry proposed for the individual projects can be frightening, since students are stimulated to dig deep and question assumptions.

Inevitably there will be some strong feelings about authority issues. Hierarchical relationships in our society are fraught with ambivalence. The professor's conventional role is that of benevolent mentor or as cold and punitive dispenser of grades—and often both at the same time. Responses to a particular professor are mixed with projected images and anticipations based on past experience with authority figures. When I renounce my institutional authority position, this does not relieve the ambivalence so much as compound it. Is this not the same old professor with a new mask? Is this a trick, a whim? And is he going to revert to his usual role whenever he tires of this one or feels challenged?

In another vein: Is the professor copping out? Is he abandoning the students when they need his authority—a bad father who is distant and uninvolved? Usually these issues concerning authority are vaguely felt and unarticulated and I am inclined to forget about them. But when the classroom seems unaccountably tense and chaotic, I often belatedly realize that unresolved issues about authority may be the cause of it. One symptom I have come to recognize is when the students are not taking responsibility for managing our classroom activities, but at the same time are resistant or disgruntled in response to suggestions that I make. On the basis of past experience, I now try to bring these issues to the surface by describing the situation as I see it: specific interactions that seem tension laden and the overall anxious mood that I sense in the class. Then I offer the conjecture that issues about authority we thought were settled may still be a problem. Sometimes the students pick up on this suggestion right away and we begin to work it out. Sometimes someone will say that he or she senses difficulties, too, but attributes them to some other conflict. At other times my suggestions will not be picked up at all—at least not at that time. A student may come back to those notions several weeks later.

My experiences along these lines have led me to believe, like Carl Rogers, that my general responsibility is to be as available as I can be, intellectually, emotionally, professionally, and personally as we struggle to develop our democratic community—but not to step in and fix it. Thus, I want to react freely in an emotional way as part of the group, trusting that these emotional responses are good barometers of the group climate—an alternative to the mechanical response of acting as an emotionally detached technical consultant.

RESOLVING THE PROFESSOR'S PROBLEMS WITH THE LACK OF TRADITIONAL AUTHORITY

In the trying to live up to the responsibilities I have set for myself and the expectations the class has for me, I inevitably stumble and blunder. So much of what I do in a democratically organized classroom is to think on my feet and to improvise. I can't protect myself from errors by having every response planned out in advance as with lectures, tightly organized syllabi, or recitation-style "discussions."

Of past mistakes I recall, most have come from my failure to integrate fully the academic and personal sides of myself. When I get carried away with an idea, I sometimes forget that I'm talking to real people, abruptly dismissing their ideas and discounting their feelings. I've noticed that this is most likely to happen when there has been some setback or hurt in my professional or personal life. I can't eliminate all such failings, but I try to recognize them once they occur. It is especially helpful if students are courageous enough to point them out to me, because then I can acknowledge them, somewhat ease the disruption or pain they've caused, clear the air, and go on.

I remember several occasions on which I acknowledged such errors. To my surprise the quality of class discussion not only recovered to its former level, but improved dramatically. Perhaps the students took this as a crucial test of my trustworthiness, or of my humanness. Perhaps also, knowing that I made mistakes, they felt safer in taking risks themselves.

THE MEDIUM AND THE MESSAGE

When I've talked with colleagues about democratic classroom experiments in the past, questions have often been raised: Aren't you sacrificing content for process? Won't students read less and won't they be deprived of your more studied and expert interpretations of the material? There are many answers to these questions. Ideally, in a self-initiated learning situation, students will be more engaged, hence motivated to read more not less. They'd be energetically searching to understand the readings and would solicit the professor's interpretation. Although this sometimes happens, there are genuine dilemmas that this ideal model overlooks.

First, there are other modes of learning. The students may be drawn to field projects or participation in and reflection on classroom process; or they may engage in retrieval of and reflection on their past experience and its political and personal meanings. Given time constraints, these approaches may compete with rather than complement book learning. I have to occasionally remind myself and the class that we can't do everything in one semester.

Second, years of experience with traditional education may have so alienated students from the written word that their first need upon being freed from compulsory reading is to avoid it. Freire describes the process of teachers "depositing" information during class and "withdrawing" it during exams as the *banking model* (Freire 1970). I'm less worried about such rebellion when I see it as part of a process, a phase if you will, rather than as a terminus. Likewise, becoming a self-starting learner, after years of banking education, will create grave anxiety for some. By the end of the course, these students may be just embarking on a wonderful voyage of discovery— one that eager educators like me would like them to be conducting all semester. But education is a lifetime pursuit, and once the student graduates, who will be lecturing to them and telling them what to read and how to analyze it? If a student has reached the threshold of genuinely self-initiated, deeply engaged lifetime learning in one semester, far from being a failure, isn't that a huge achievement?

My response has been, and continues to be, a firm commitment to trust and to join the students in whatever path they are following, in becoming equal partners in the democratic community of learning. In the past, whenever I wavered in that commitment, I would reread Carl Rogers to remind myself of the wonderfully positive outcomes that flow from such trust and commitment and of his account of the intrinsic motivations of people toward self-actualization—not as isolated atomistic selves, but as selves-in-relation to a social and natural world (Rogers 1961).

When wavering in this resolve, I consider the consequences of the alternative. Suppose I accept that I am entitled to use the power that this hierarchical system gives me to guide/compel students in the righteous path that they should follow, because I know better than they the map of that path. The bottom line of this method is that I don't trust the students, and I don't trust democracy. My actions teach exactly the opposite of what my words are saying. And most of the students will be confirmed in accepting the existing order, even while they read all sorts of critical and progressive thought. The subgroup who are influenced by the readings and lectures toward a democratic and progressive political outlook—or who came to the course already holding such a view—will, unfortunately, be encouraged to become a new generation of elitists like myself. I'm more aware of and less comfortable with such self-contradictions than I used to be.

THEORIES OF KNOWLEDGE AND THEIR RELATION TO DEMOCRATIC EDUCATION

It is often said that truth is not a matter to be decided by majorities, or to put it more crudely, by mob rule. Thus, the university is exempted from democracy. It should be ruled by standards of validity, logic, method, evidence, objectivity, impartiality, and so on. This creed also holds that the faculty members should be the guardians of those standards. The faculty members are also the bearers of a stock of validated knowledge that has already been accumulated and it is their duty to dispense this to the students. To propose democratic classrooms, then, requires us to challenge the theories of knowledge on which traditional educational practices rest.

The predominant theory of knowledge, which clearly and unflinchingly supports the argument against democratic classrooms, is positivism. This atomistic, empiricist school of thought came, in the last century, to generally dominate Anglo-American philosophy on science, social science, and knowledge. During its peak years, roughly from World War I until past midcentury, alternative traditions—for example, American pragmatism, and several varieties of continental thought—were pushed to the margins. But the positivist view is very much in retreat today, at least among those who have taken the trouble to keep up with the theoretical literature. The publication of Thomas Kuhn's *The Structure of Scientific Revolutions* (1962), marked the turning point, though it is best understood as representative of a broad wave of change rather than the single key factor. A range of highly regarded contemporary views that evidence and knowledge are contextual and perspectival, rather than universal, as previously understood, now exists. Standards are understood to be, in this view, more internal to particular schools of thought and thus subject to evolution, rather than universal and fixed for all time. Knowledge is also understood more as embodied and linked to practice, rather than distinct from, and having authority over, experience.

It would seem that these developments favor both the democratization of inquiry and education and participation over reception. Professors, in this view, can no longer be simply the guardians of universal standards and objective knowledge. They are situated in their own particular paradigms, cultural backgrounds, and life histories. They are still important contributors to the ongoing development and evolution of knowledge and standards, but not privileged possessors of verities etched in stone. Classrooms can then be seen as sites of practices that engage students and teachers in a common experience. And students, rather than being seen as blank slates, can be understood as coming to the classroom with their own unique perspectives and embodied knowledge. I believe that the new theories of knowledge do, indeed, open the way to democratization of education. For the most part, however, they have not been interpreted this way. How paradoxical and how tragic—at least in my view. Possible sources of that seeming paradox will now be explored.

For one thing, the new views still have limited reach within the academic world. Despite the excitement generated by these new developments among a significant minority of scholars and the swift decline of support for positivism among specialists in the philosophy of science, many social scientists have remained blissfully ignorant of them. Insulated by their specialized research focus, many have paid scant attention. Others have acknowledged the new ideas but have made merely ad hoc adjustments in their positivist programs.

Even among those who have adopted the new theories of knowledge, however, there is little inclination to draw conclusions calling for democratization of the classroom. For some who have adopted the new outlook, this is simply another theory, another item that the professor feels entitled to convey to the student in the traditional manner. There is no link made between theory and practice. For another group the new theory is interpreted in a nihilistic fashion. No political position and no way of relating to students can be shown to be better than any other, so why not simply go on as before?

Beyond these failures to fully grapple and experiment with the theory, I will suggest that there are indeed limitations within the theory itself, such that it fails to strongly imply democratization of classrooms. I will now explore these limitations in contrast with a humanistic and transformational alternative. This humanistic approach seems to me both more theoretically adequate and more democratic in its implications.

The recognition that knowledge is situated opens the way to a conception of knowledge as intertwined with practice, which has profound implications for the classroom. But contemporary theories of knowledge don't take us all the way. Much of current theory is, in actuality, highly intellectualized and cut off from political, educational, and even personal life. Aside from sociological explanation in terms of the isolated and elite status of the professorate and the dark times of the post–Vietnam War era, I am searching for explanations intrinsic to the theory itself.

First, it seems to me that experimentation follows naturally from understanding that knowledge is embodied and linked to practice, but this link is broken if one's material of study is limited to fixed texts. Interpretation has been seen as the primary alternative to positivist social science, and the model for interpretation has come from literary theory and historiography in which the texts to be studied are artifacts produced in the past and in their final form. One can no longer intervene in the ongoing process of the production of these texts, as one might intervene, for example, in a process of community development that, as a political scientist, one is researching. The interpretive approach also draws heavily from anthropology, in which, interestingly, experimental intervention is possible but is enjoined on ethical grounds. Having these disciplines as models perhaps explains in part why postempiricist social scientists still seek to study society as if from outside, though in fact they are inextricably immersed within it.

Second, I sense that, for some scholars, the concept of practice is still severely constricted by the survival of a Marxist-Leninist conception: The only practice worthy of the name is mass political action—indeed, the action of a revolutionary party, and one that has a very real chance of defeating the old order and winning power over the state. By this standard we live in a time in which there is no political practice and theory must become a self-enclosed enterprise.

Third, the breakdown of the old certainties has been taken by many as leading to ethical skepticism and even nihilism. One cannot act without purposes one believes to be good or right, so one is incapable of acting at all. This way leads to paralysis and embittered impotence.

Presuming I am right that any or all of these aspects of theory contribute to the failure to act, to experiment, and hence to bring democratic theory into classroom practice, I offer the following theoretical counterproposals.

First, social inquiry is not simply a matter of interpretation. It is inherently experimental. Theory is nothing if it is not an account of practice. And theory is not believable unless it is tested in practice. What is more, inquiry must constantly be searching for new knowledge, or it decays into what William James called "inert ideas." This new knowledge is discovered in experience that enriches our reading of texts. What we find in those texts is valued and validated insofar as it feeds back into action. I believe that the classroom is indeed a site of meaningful action.

Second, in contrast to the Marxist-Leninist view I urge the alternative that: (1) every time we undertake purposive action involving other people this is a matter of practice—as in the views of Dewey and much of contemporary feminism, and (2) that even in dark times our practice does matter and has a bearing upon the future. We need, in Gramsci's words, "pessimism of the intellect but optimism of the will." From this perspective, our work in the classroom is practice. Whether this practice is consistent with our theories and aspirations concerning democracy is of crucial importance. If we teach about democracy in a structure that is undemocratic, will the students not learn the experiential lesson rather than the textual one? Will they be paralyzed by the contradiction between the two? Meanwhile our own development as democratic theorists is in danger of producing sterile abstractions, not enlivened and corrected by democratic practice. Finally, the fundamental ethical challenge of consistency between ends and means will be evaded.

Third, ethical skepticism can liberate our action from dogmatism, a curse of past political movements on the left, but it need not lead to nihilism and inaction. Indeed despair about any sustainable notion of what is good and right is the reverse of the old absolutist notion that there is a fixed truth to be discovered in matters of ethics. Furthermore, there is no escape from choosing. Inaction is itself a form of action on behalf of the established system. The genuine alternative to absolutism and relativism is the search for the good and the right in an experimental spirit by democratic communities (Bernstein 1983). Since ethical understandings are not absolute, no professor or other authority is licensed to be the sole purveyor of it, and inquiry becomes truly collaborative.

KNOWLEDGE AND THE SELF

Current theories of knowledge can also open the way to fresh thought on the relationship of knowledge and the self, with democratic implications. But this promise has not always been fulfilled. I propose that knowledge only exists insofar as it is embodied not just in acts but in the selves who perform those acts. Indeed, as Dewey suggests, one key aspect of the constitution of selfhood is meaning acquired through experience. To acquire significant new knowledge, then, is to change—to become in some degree a new self. In this view, the very nature of selfhood is process; a self that is not growing is already beginning to disintegrate. Recognition from others, some degree of security within one's social group, and the stimulation and challenge of dealing with real issues and choices are necessary for growth. High levels of anxiety, though they occasionally drive a person to great achievements, usually lead to a defensive quest for certainty and stasis. A democratic classroom, like a democratic society, can provide the needed support, recognition, responsibility, and challenge—an optimal environment for human learning and growth.

This affirmation of selfhood is not an endorsement of the model of the bourgeois subject—a unitary, transparent, self-sufficient, and wholly autonomous agent. Without denying our multiplicity and heteronomy, I endorse the democratic project of working toward integration of the self and toward autonomous, responsible choice. I can act on the democratic faith that there is a core of selfhood in which this project can take root. This is not a blind faith, but a working commitment that enables me to engage in democratic practice and to test this belief in experience. The denial of autonomous selfhood, on the other hand, by giving us reasons not to respect the selves of others, can be a self-fulfilling prophecy. The conscious voluntary self, as Dewey puts it, is forged out of the experience of initiative, choice, and action—and of reflection upon them. Our hierarchical society and educational system has thwarted such engagement, and much contemporary theory, no matter how radical it purports to be, fails to confront the hierarchical position of the theorists themselves.

Much of contemporary theory has taken a very different view of knowledge and the self. Knowledge is considered a product of society as a whole and existing independently of any individual. Rather than creating, possessing, and embodying such knowledge, our selves are possessed by it and it creates itself through us. Our selves are constructed. Hence such concepts as "decentering of the subject" and "deconstruction of the bourgeois self" have emerged. This emergence has been liberating insofar as it calls our attention to the way society has shaped what we naively think are our autonomous identities and values. It has been liberating in calling us to recognize that in response to external forces we have disowned a substantial part of what does or could go on within us. Unfortunately, this theory tells us only how the self can be deconstructed, but not, if you will, how it can be reconstructed. Thus, in its own way, it maintains the status quo ante.

The theory has indeed been pushed to the point where there are no selves at all, only social forces. There is no coherence in the self, only fragments overlaid with illusions of unity based on denial of multiplicity. This "antihumanism"—as some structuralist and poststructuralist theorists call it—seems to me to be more than just a theoretical posture; it gets carried out in human relationships. It seems to have absolved some scholars and teachers from regarding students and colleagues as human beings to whom one has the moral obligations of respect and care. These ethically perverse consequences of theory serve as more reason to question its adequacy and to reconsider a humanistic account of knowledge and the self.

In the humanistic account, the democratic classroom involves our full participation as people, not just partial participation as thinkers, or role players, or as workers at tasks. Thus, from the side of practice, it also calls for an understanding of personalities, of selves. I suspect that one unexpressed reason for the lack of consideration of democratic pedagogy, however much theory may press us in that direction, is that many of us feel unprepared to deal with the complexity, ambiguity, and difficulty of personal relationships in the classroom. Some of us perhaps would find appropriate such metaphors as *quicksand* or *mine field*. Structure and centralized authority in the classroom permit the avoidance of such dangers. But if knowledge and self are inseparable, then we evade such personal encounters at the cost of limiting how much we can teach. More fundamentally, we limit the development of our theory and knowledge.

It seems to me that one of the major premises of academic life and scholarship, shared by traditional and contemporary theories alike, is that our winged intellects can fly free of our constrained and flawed selves. This may indeed be the case for limited spans of subject matter for limited periods of time. In the long run, I think it is an illusion that impoverishes our knowledge, as well as stunts our growth as people and thwarts the realization of democracy. Perhaps the separation of knowledge and the self is the last stubborn, entrenched prejudice of the ivory tower, the last Maginot Line of the old theory of knowledge.

RADICAL PEDAGOGY

The new theories of knowledge have been employed by a significant group of left-oriented faculty members as justifying a radical pedagogy. On the whole this is a welcome development, but to the extent that nondemocratic or antidemocratic implications have crept in, they need to be confronted. The theoretical reasoning behind such disregard for democracy, as I understand it goes like this: If knowledge is situated, this provides a wedge for critiquing the existing curriculum as ideological, not objective. The conventional and establishment theories, texts, and claims of knowledge can be seen as rationalizations for the drastic inequalities of the American political and economic system. Those who present this critical view operate, however, at a severe disadvantage. The mainstream view, after all, is reinforced by the mass media, by primary and secondary education, and indeed by most college courses. Thus, it is argued by some, we are morally bound to use the one asset that is at our disposal, our power in the classroom, to challenge the prevailing views and to provide compelling alternatives. By providing— even imposing—such alternatives, it is said, one is liberating the students, not dominating them. This last step seems to me to be a perilous slip of both logic and ethics. I propose, to the contrary, that using professorial power to preach progressive views endorses by example the existing hierarchical structure, or, at best, produces some new elitist radicals. Conversely, the very act of renouncing that power and encouraging students to govern their classroom is a potent critique-in-practice of the antidemocratic system.

Such radical educators also object to the "expressivist" and humanist views that emphasize helping students to find their own voice and to actualize their own selves. The voices and selves that will be expressed in student-initiated learning and student-directed classrooms, in this view, will not come from some imagined, authentic core of autonomous individuality and intrinsic humanity, but instead will be recitations of conventional societal beliefs and attitudes—the voices of elitism, consumerism, sexism, and racism. On the contrary, I propose, that unless students are given a chance to verbalize the ideas implanted in them by society and to expose these undemocratic views and critiques, they will not have the chance for reflection and development of more considered, voluntarily chosen positions. To override such voices is likely to push them underground only to resurface later or to create disciples whose progressive ideas are not coupled with personal autonomy and empowerment.

CONCLUSION

When I accept a transformational and humanistic account of connections of theory/practice and knowledge/self, then the case for democratization of the classroom becomes compelling. It seems impossible, in this light, to teach effectively about democracy unless the students and I are free to experience it, to learn to function in it, and to grow and change through this experience. The old rationale that students acquire more knowledge in the teacher-controlled classroom collapses because I have a very different account of knowledge—an account in which book learning is important as it helps us understand our experience, but is not independent of such experience. Ideas don't become knowledge except by being embodied in practice and in consequent transformations of the self. This is the theory of knowledge that seems to me to be the best fruit of recent theoretical inquiry. At the same time, it is a theory of knowledge with profoundly democratic implications.

REFERENCES

Bernstein, Richard. 1983. *Beyond Objectivism and Relativism: Science, Hermeneutics, and Praxis*. Philadelphia: University of Pennsylvania Press.

Boydston, J., ed. 1981–1992. *John Dewey: The Later Works: 1925–1953*. 17 vols. Carbondale, Ill.: Southern Illinois University Press.

Dewey, John. 1939. "Creative Democracy." In *John Dewey: The Political Writings,*
    ed. D. Morris and I. Shapiro. Indianapolis: Hackett Publishing Company.
Freire, Paulo. 1970. *Pedagogy of the Oppressed.* New York: Continuum Publishing
    Co.
Gandhi, M. 1951. *Nonviolent Resistance.* New York: Schocken Books.
Kuhn, Thomas. 1970. *The Structure of Scientific Revolutions.* 2nd ed. Chicago: Uni-
    versity of Chicago Press.
———. 1977. "Objectivity, Values, and Theory Choice." In *The Essential Tension.*
    Chicago: University of Chicago Press.
Miller, Anne. 1981. *The Drama of the Gifted Child.* New York: Basic Books.
Rogers, Carl. 1961. *On Becoming a Person: A Therapist's View of Psychotherapy.* Bos-
    ton: Houghton Mifflin.

2

Personal Empowerment

Louis Herman

Shortly after I began teaching, I had a moment of shared insight with the students of my class. It occurred to me that instead of regarding teaching as a means to support my graduate research, I could turn it into a form of Socratic inquiry—participatory fieldwork for a Ph.D. in politics. I started using my classroom as an informal laboratory for experimenting and reflecting on the primal convergence between democracy and the search for meaning in community. The collaborative dialectic of teaching and learning was itself a crucial component of the "good society." Today, looking around at the dismal situation of both teaching and democracy in America, I feel I might have stumbled onto something of benefit to others.

SOCRATES IN THE CLASSROOM

I arrived almost twenty years ago as a foreign graduate student in an unusually supportive American political science department. In my second semester I was honored and a little stunned to find myself as a teaching assistant charged with designing my own introductory course in political science. This particularly impressed me since I had never actually taken an undergraduate social science course.

After enduring a semester in daily terror of being exposed as a fraud, I abandoned pretense and admitted (at least to myself) solidarity with my students in their ignorance. Since my economic survival depended on continuing to teach successfully, I did everything I could to coax honest feedback from my students. Out of necessity, preparing for class time became the center of my intellectual life. This shift in attention from my teachers to my students was reinforced by a growing dissatisfaction with the current state of my academic discipline as a framework for "the search for meaning" that had initially attracted me to the study of politics.

My confidence improved with the discovery that, for the most part, students were touchingly eager to help me teach them something meaningful. An unexpected benefit of this initiation by the uninitiated was my rediscovery of some humbling Socratic wisdom concerning the convergence between education and democracy.

I remember well the moment of mutual illumination while wrestling in class with one of the more Zen-like passages of Plato's *Republic*. It occurred after I had been teaching for a few semesters. The puzzling passage occurred in the chapter "The Good as the Highest Object of Knowledge." Why does Socrates one moment insist that "the essential nature of the Good" is the most important philosophical question and the next moment refuse to answer his own question, apologizing profusely for his ignorance? And then why does he suddenly change his mind and define what he has just claimed he does not know, "the Good is that which makes knowledge possible"?[1]

As I questioned the class about this paradox, an image of the give-and-take between Socrates and his companion Glaucon became superimposed on the frank discussion that we had been enjoying in the classroom. In a flash of self-reflection I realized that Socrates was trying to provoke Glaucon to reflect upon the process in which he had been engaged. He was trying to get Glaucon to realize that the essence of the Good—the source of knowledge of how to live the best life possible—inheres in what I and my class were already doing, the collaborative, face-to-face, dialectical search for knowledge of the best way to live. In a real sense, Socrates did not have "the answer."

PEDAGOGY OF THE OPPRESSED—TYRANNY OF THE EXPERT

In the introduction to this book, Becker and Couto cite the work of the Brazilian educator Paulo Freire to critique the prevailing "banking deposit" model of education as not only ineffective but also one that disempowers the student as a political agent.[2] Caspary also cited Freire to make the same point. Many of us seem to recognize that the existing mode, for the most part, assumes the teacher as full of knowledge and the student an empty receptacle to be filled with regular deposits of facts. All that is required of the student is accurate bookkeeping. The banking model denies knowledge as a relational process of connecting parts to wholes, in which the primary connection is between the experience of the student (of which the teacher is initially ignorant) and the experience of the teacher (of which the student is equally initially ignorant).

By contrast according to the deep dimension of the Socratic example— both participants are required to recognize mutual, if asymmetric, igno- rance. Student and teacher participate in a dialectical search for meaning that requires, in some real sense, the teacher to learn and the student to teach. It is for this reason I believe that Socrates avoided lecturing, had no library, and never founded an academy. Instead, he insisted on the superi- ority of face-to-face discussion in which reference to personal experience was direct and unavoidable.

It was Plato who froze Socrates' discussions into texts, founded the first university in the Grove of Academus, and envisioned the elitist republic. One of the most important recent works on Socrates is emphatic on this point: "To confine as Plato does (in Books IV and VII of *The Republic*) moral inquiry to a tiny elite, is to obliterate the Socratic vision which opens up the philosophic life to all" (Vlastos 1991:18). Despite his much-noted critique of Athenian democracy, it is Socrates who embodies a profoundly democratic method in the philosophical quest for enlightenment. Con- versely, he insists on the necessity of bringing a philosophical attitude to political democracy—that until those in authority and power love wisdom and justice more than wealth and honors, the world will never see an end to needless suffering.

I'm not suggesting giving up literature (or electronics) and regressing to an oral culture. Nor am I endorsing the know-nothing relativism (today sometimes identified with procedural democracy) that assumes all opinions are equally worthwhile. My point is to provide some practically relevant theory concerning the connection between an enlightening pedagogy and democracy.

Since the 1960s, the steady growth of research on teaching has provided considerable empirical confirmation of Freire's theoretical attack on the banking model. The evidence accumulates for the cynical view that in most cases a lecture involves the transmission of information from the notes of the instructor to the notes of the students without passing through the minds of either. Typically during the fifty-minute lecture, there is a five- minute settling in period, then students assimilate material and attentively take notes for the next five minutes. Ten to twenty minutes into the lecture, confusion and boredom set in. Retention and comprehension decline further and remain low until about five minutes before the end of class when stu- dents are apparently revived by the knowledge that the lecture will soon be over (Bonwell and Eison 1991:9). Most of us probably have uncomfortable memories of being either victim or perpetrator (or both) of the sort of lecture described by Coolie Verner and Gary Dickenson, as cited in Bonwell and Eison (1991).

Ten percent of the audience displayed signs of inattention within 15 minutes. After 18 minutes one third of the audience and 10 percent of the platform guests were fidgeting. At 35 minutes everyone was inattentive: at 45 minutes, trance was more noticeable than fidgeting; at 47 minutes some were asleep and at least one was reading. A casual check 24 hours later revealed that the audience recalled only insignificant details, [which] were generally wrong.[3]

Strangely, teaching continues to remain immune from the rich and growing body of research by education specialists. In the natural sciences, discussion is hardly attempted until the student is involved in research. Even in the humanities and social sciences, the vast majority of undergraduate class time still consists of the instructor lecturing from notes with no more than a few minutes at the end for questions and discussion. A study of 155 class sessions from 47 classes revealed the time spent on questions ranged from 1 to 10 percent of class time. On average, 82 percent of questions were on the lowest cognitive level, requiring only memorization. Only 2 percent required valuative thinking (Eison, Janzow, and Bonwell 1990:87). Another piece of research on 550 lecture hours showed that the average wait-time after the instructor asked a question was about 1.5 seconds before the question would be repeated or changed. When the instructor tolerated silence for three to five seconds, several interesting changes occurred. The number of higher-order responses increased as did the number of student questions and the amount of student-to-student conversation (Rowe 1974a, 1974b).

In the hands of a skilled practitioner, the lecture can be uniquely effective in generating enthusiasm for a subject, organizing material, communicating recent research, and, in some cases, communicating information. However, it is now almost axiomatic in the educational research literature that "learning is not a spectator sport." There is near consensus among the researchers that effective learning, particularly concerning emotional and higher-order intellectual development, requires interactive and participatory strategies.

At its most basic level, active learning simply involves the participant engaging the material in ways other than listening to a lecture, although some lecturers insist that listening is an active process. Active strategies generally acknowledge and use the collective experience of the group and tend to be more concerned with influencing attitudes and values and developing skills rather than in transmitting information. Active strategies also provide participants with immediate feedback from the instructor and other group members.

Why then does lecture dominate class time and remain synonymous with university teaching? The problem is deeper than simple ignorance of alternatives or the comforts of habit. The content-heavy, banking model of teaching is supported by an authoritarian, positivistic epistemology deeply rooted in the institutions of modernity. It persists despite, and perhaps because of, decades of academic "deconstruction" of modernity.

In part, the reason for this persistence is that a meaningful political education requires a "constructive" epistemology in addition to the overused armory of analytical and critical tools. Deconstructionism, despite its hostility to the hegemony of European institutions, remains, like positivism, rooted in the metaphysics of modernity specifically the Newtonian/Cartesian emphasis on analysis, skepticism, and critique. Both positivism and post-modernism ignore (for ostensibly different reasons) the re-*construction* of meaning as central to political inquiry. Many postmodernists become unconscious victims of the ironic reversals they celebrate as they perpetuate this negative one-sidedness of modernity by deconstructing everything in sight. The resulting fragmentation of thought reinforces the power of the specialist and the rule of the expert.

The narrowness of vision in all areas of life, a by-product of the industrial division of labor, is, as Adam Smith insisted, the short-term recipe for productivity. Thus, there is little compensating demand or reward for the generalist. The university collaborates by following the bottom line of the academic market. Inquiry splinters into ever smaller marketable fragments. With the loss of the incentive to integrate knowledge goes the possibility for approaching a shared vision of the good of the whole. Policy formulation and implementation is increasingly confined to professional administrators, economists, scientists, lawyers, business leaders, and professional soldiers. Some political scientists, following Seymour Martin Lipset's analysis, even celebrate nonvoting as the triumph of a professional political culture. We have now reached a situation in which presidential elections are television dramas in which the best and the brightest media consultants manipulate the lowest common denominator—and almost half the electorate stays home switching channels.

I believe the real challenge in teaching political science is now one of reconstruction—building a democratic, intellectual culture in which the citizen is both empowered *and motivated* to participate in decisions concerning the good of all. I contend that the honest back and forth of Socratic discussion is at the heart of such a culture—a collaborative search for the good of all—both in society and in the soul of the seeker.

How does one go about creating a genuine Socratic culture within a competitive, hierachical system where a would-be Socrates has the power to pass or fail the other discussants? The most direct response is to make the Socratic agenda—independent, thoughtful, questioning—explicit as *one* standard for grading. I will first try to clarify elements of such a democratic pedagogy and then deal with the bottom line of grading.

AUTHENTIC DISCUSSION AND THE RETURN TO EXPERIENCE

Direct reference to experience has long been labeled "subjective" and excluded from higher education. This situation persists despite volumes of sophisticated, epistemological clarification demonstrating how all knowledge claims are inevitably contextual, rooted in the life world of unique individuals. Reference to personal experience is also a crucial part of democratic education as empowerment. This reference can be clarified for classroom use, without a fog of jargon, by placing the Socratic method alongside its primal roots in the oral-experiential traditions of hunting-and-gathering societies.

One successful teacher at a small liberal arts college admitted that "it took me twenty years of college teaching to allow myself to see the fear on the faces of my students" (Lawry 1990). People will not generally participate in class or in public life when they feel they might be cut down, graded down, or ridiculed for their contribution. Genuine Socratic discussion is possible only to the degree that mutual trust and respect prevail.

The most common complaint I hear from teachers attempting to move away from a lecture-based pedagogy describes the difficulty they find in getting students to have a real discussion "like pulling teeth." After analyzing hundreds of student evaluations (my own and those of my peers as a member of personnel committees) I am convinced that the vast majority of students are ashamed of their ignorance, fear public humiliation at the hands of the professor, and know that the bottom line is giving the instructor what he or she expects.

The intellectual culture in general, and the literature on active learning in particular, lacks a theoretically developed, action-oriented participatory epistemology. A substantial transformation of teaching, learning, and higher education (as well as of society in general) will take place only when teachers have a better understanding of why participatory strategies are generally more truth-generating and empowering than passive lecturing. In particular, instructors need to understand that masochistic altruism is not a necessary condition for change. Benefits from student participation accrue as much *to teachers* as to their students.

If we assume that the collective is composed of human beings who are all moral agents capable of significant choice, then the instructor can no longer have all the answers. Because the focus of inquiry is the Socratic quest for the-good-of-*all*, every individual's self-understanding at any moment becomes relevant "data." After all, as the classical polis recognized, the good society was in part to be measured by the quality of life (the virtue) of unique individuals. In such an inquiry, living, investigating, and then sharing one's own story becomes both method and content, means and ends.

The Socratic allegory of the cave provides an appropriately venerable metaphor for such a return to experience. Those imprisoned in the cave have their experience of reality confined by their chains. The "philosopher," once a prisoner himself, breaks his chains, turns around, sees the source of the shadows projected on the wall and then continues to expand his experience by stepping out of the cave to explore the world. When he returns, his understanding of his own nature in relation to the whole is enlarged, but his success in rejoining the world of the prisoners is impaired. He has to adapt to the dim light of the cave. He struggles to remember what he knew as a prisoner. Instead of receiving him as a guru, his fellow prisoners chortle at his clumsy attempts to regain his old place as a prisoner.

The challenge for the returning philosopher, then, is to symbolically and imaginatively connect the experience they all manifestly share (life in the cave) with the enlightenment that the philosopher alone has experienced. Such a process of imaginatively and symbolically enlarging one's understanding in the interests of living more copiously, implies the give and take of discussion in which all participants collaborate in building linguistic bridges between their distant islands of experience. The collective search for the truths of the best way to live focuses this exchange. We are all both enlightened and blinded by our trajectory through life—a trajectory that is always more or less unique and more or less shared. Relative to the life experience of others, we are all philosophers in caves.

For example, when I left my native South Africa to live in England at the age of thirteen, I left a cave of bitter racial intolerance for the politeness of English liberalism. But I simultaneously entered an urban cave shaded from the vigor and illumination of an outdoor African childhood. The more we can share in the lives of others (especially those who differ from us radically), the greater the possibility of an expanded world of symbolically shared experience. The more copious our experience of life, the less likely we are to fall for the ideological prisons of modernity and the more we move toward the possibilities of the best life possible *together* in community. As I moved back and forth between Africa and England, I became more critical of the ethnocentric excesses of both societies—yet at the same time my appreciation for "the good, the true, and the beautiful" in both intensified. If we are to do more than pay lip service to Socrates as the paradigmatic figure for politics, we need to behave differently in the classroom.

The oral culture of tribal societies helps make more explicit what is still implicit in the Socratic example. The traditional teaching of the medicine wheel of the Plains Indians is particularly appropriate for reinforcing the importance of face-to-face discussion in a class on democratic politics. At the same time, it integrates a multicultural approach at the most fundamental level.

The medicine wheel as explained by the contemporary Cheyenne shaman Hyemeohsts Storm, is a mandala—a cross circumscribed by a circle—the oldest known and most widely distributed sacred symbol (Storm 1972). "Sun wheel" petroglyphs have been found dating back to Paleolithic times and more recently in such diverse settings as the healing ritual of Navaho sand paintings, European alchemy, and as objects of meditation in Tibetan Buddhism (Jung 1973). In every context the mandala represents the whole as a balancing of the pairs of binary opposites: male-female, child-adult, day-night, summer-winter, human-animal, mind-body, and so forth. According to Storm, the wheel at its most inclusive represents the universe macrocosm. Every pebble, every blade of grass, every animal, every human being and every tribe, culture, and civilization has a place on the wheel. Of all living creatures, only humans are not born with an understanding of their place and their limits—how to "give away." Humans are alone among the creatures in being "determiners," yet they are for the most part ignorant of their part in the drama of being and thus constantly prone to hubris. The main purpose of teaching, then, is to facilitate the quest that arises from this primal existential anxiety. What is the best way to live? Isn't that essentially Socratic?

Storm then asks the reader to imagine the medicine wheel as a group of people sitting in a circle on the prairie trying to come to agreement. Assume that the group is asked to decide the meaning of an object, for example, a painted drum, placed in the middle of the circle. In such a situation the wheel symbolizes the primal social whole—the Socratic circle of discussants. As each person in the group tries to elucidate the meaning of the drum, it becomes clear that the description will vary according to one's position in the circle. In addition, the meaning of the object will vary according to each person's powers of observation, capacity to communicate, and, ultimately, accumulated life experience. Should the object be a person or an idea instead of a drum? The variety and complexity of interpretations would increase exponentially. The structure of the circle also makes it clear that the larger, truer meaning depends on an interpretive synthesis of as many diverse contributions as possible. Once again, we are struck by the Socratic insight that the quest for meaning is quintessentially a democratic and communal enterprise.

The individual's search for truth and meaning requires moving beyond one's starting point on the wheel—to become "what you are not"—a move toward wholeness through affirming opposites and crossing boundaries. Since everyone's starting point on the wheel is different, each individual follows a unique path toward greater wholeness. The similarity with the Socratic method is striking and suggests the possibility of a primal, multi-civilizational journey toward truth that is fundamental to the human condition.[4] Questioning the status quo, one's starting point on the wheel, is a first step for both methods. According to Storm, "questioning turns the wheel." Like the Socratic method, one seeks a path of new experiences guided by the imaginative attempt to build verbal (symbolic) bridges between previously disparate worlds of experience.

Both methods teach that rather than submit to our tendency to avoid conflict, we should seek out those who disagree. Let those who see life from a different position on the wheel be teachers for us. By the same token, we become teachers for them as we approach the ideal of an emancipated community of truth seekers.

As well as the macrocosm, the wheel also symbolizes the microcosm—

the individual's journey toward wholeness—psychic integration of as wide a range of human experiences as possible. The story of the Lakota medicine man Lame Deer exemplifies such an integrated life of disparate elements such as preacher, spud-picker, cowhand, clown, sign painter, healer, bootlegger, president of the Indian YMCA. "I managed to be both a heathen and a holy man, a fugitive and a pursuer, a lawman and an outlaw. I was uneducated but soaked up knowledge like a sponge" (Storm 1972:80). Lame Deer emphasizes how the alchemy of fusing opposites amplifies the quest for wisdom. "A medicine man shouldn't be a saint. He should experience and feel all the ups and downs, the despair and joy, the magic and the reality, the courage and the fear, of his people. . . . You have to be God and the devil, both of them. Being a good medicine man means being right in the midst of the turmoil, not shielding yourself from it" (Storm 1972: 79).

The wisdom of the healer is the wisdom of the whole—a teaching that expresses the Anglo-Saxon roots of "health" in "hal" meaning "whole."[5] Lame Deer's unreserved love for the contradictions of life can help move students to open themselves up to relating to whatever is the tabooed opposite of their own laboriously constructed identity—radical/conservative, capitalist/socialist, modern/primitive, European/non-European, and so forth. The lesson for classroom discussion is to risk openness to the perspectives of those with whom we disagree with most. Gentle reminders of Lame Deer's attitude can help students disagree on important issues with a minimum of anger and insult. One can imagine how a democracy composed of such balanced individuals might be better capable of sustaining the good society and administering a humanistic justice than the callow citizens of Socrates' Athens or the one-dimensional bureaucrats of the modern state.

STORYTELLING—HONEST TALK ABOUT FIRST THINGS

The first step in putting such an epistemology into practice with a new class is to do the polite thing by introducing oneself. I open class by telling my story, how I moved through several continents, cultures, and professions to end up pursuing the good life at the University of Hawaii. In so doing, I can relate my interpretation of the discipline's tradition to the trajectory of my life up to the present, shared moment. What I have to offer, inclusive though it is, remains always limited. No one has the last word as long as there is still more life to be lived. My authority as instructor is simply another position on the medicine wheel.

To legitimate this personalization of the political, I refer to the Socratic example and the allegory of the cave. I take advantage of the power of the picture by showing a ten-minute animated video of the allegory in which Orson Welles paraphrases Plato's text. Moving from the verbal to the visual helps level the intellectual playing field. The literal image of the cave, with additional references to the medicine wheel, makes it possible for relatively unreflective and semiliterate students to participate in an epistemological discussion. Making the epistemology explicit helps distinguish mutual disclosure from "touchy-feely" encounter groups and dignifies it as part of a shared quest for the good of all. The point is quite easy to grasp—all knowledge claims concerning the good life need to be understood in relation to the concrete experiences of unique individuals.

The class then moves into a circle—a partial enactment of the medicine wheel as a political community—and each person shares as much of their political autobiography as he or she wishes. Sharing fragments of one's story establishes the initial coordinates of the classroom culture. We know to whom we are talking. Others have some clue as to where we are coming from. This elementary condition of communication is often obscured by the academic requirement of scientific objectivity. Personal introductions elevate self-awareness by making vivid the variety of paths that have brought the individuals to this shared experience. The direct reference to experience is both empowering (everyone has some unique experience of "life") and humbling (whatever we know is not the last word). In addition, the focus on the personal exposes and legitimates the emotional subtext of all knowledge claims. Our values and the origins of our action come from our deepest emotions. Emotions need to be recognized and expressed before detached evaluation can take place. When students recognize that it is the experienced quality of life that is ultimately the issue, their commitment to the class intensifies dramatically. With feelings activated, the intellect follows.

During introductions I encourage some spontaneous reactions, comments, and questions. The model of the clinically impassive group facilitator defeats the Socratic purpose of personalizing the political. It is hardly encouraging to make some heartfelt declaration to a group of strangers and be met with stone faces devoid of the slightest twitch of recognition or comprehension. Creating a class culture of spontaneous sharing is a political art that, in its appreciation for the individual and the unique, defies strict rules of procedure. It involves the instructor providing a model for appreciative, honest, and spontaneous reactions to personal contributions, without succumbing to quick judgments or the temptation to tell another story.

To minimize stage fright, I might leave introductions for the second class and ask students to prepare a written version of their story that they can read from if they wish. Teaching in Hawaii, where there are dramatic cultural differences in attitudes toward participation and disclosure, has taught me to be sensitive to reticent students. I offer students the option of confining their introduction to "what I feel about politics" and "what I would like to learn from this course." With special permission, written responses are acceptable in place of public declarations. However, I make it clear that the capacity to stand up in front of a group of relative strangers and make a case for one's opinion is fundamental to strong democracy, and a goal of the class is, in fact, to provide coaching in that art. It has been a source of ongoing amazement and pleasure for me to witness a growing capacity in my students for honest disclosure and sharing—the kernel of a democratic class culture.

The written responses also have a very practical benefit for class preparation by making it possible for me to quickly get to know the students as a collection of unique individuals. I can then fine tune the course content appropriately. For example, it would be foolhardy to deal with Vietnam and neoimperialism without relating it to the testimony of any military veterans in the class. Since our student body is nontraditional—the average age is thirty-three—there is a wealth of life experience relevant to just about every topic covered in politics.

Such an approach makes lecturing more of a creative challenge. I have found lectures, if well prepared, optimize learning when confined to about one-third of class time, with the remainder divided between audiovisual material and discussion. Although such personalized crafting of the lecture component is initially labor intensive, as the semester progresses and the class becomes something of an organic community, I can move into a more intuitive and relaxed style of lecturing.

Without this personal component, techniques for participation remain techniques—modes of manipulation. Treating people as interchangeable units is a denial of the central teaching of the medicine wheel and the central value of direct democracy—the notion of the citizen as a moral agent. There is no shortcut to valuing the contribution of each unique individual. Uniqueness—being one's own person and living one's own life—is the inevitable outcome of exercising our freedom and capacity for significant choice. Such caring tends to come naturally as one listens to students' stories, with the big payoff being the sense of mutual understanding.

After long neglect by academia, storytelling is now being recognized as a fundamental mode of human cognition.[6] It obliges philosophy to root itself in the primal discipline of putting words to experience, what Max Horkheimer referred to as "the conscious effort to knit all our knowledge and insight into a linguistic structure in which things are called by their right names" (Horkheimer 1974:179). Unlike "theory," which is characteristically atemporal and abstract, the story can deal with unique events as they transpire over time. The story is thus necessary for describing and explaining developmental processes (including learning itself). As modern psychoanalysis has rediscovered, reflecting on one's story can help recover what one has been punished into forgetting. Forbidden impulses can be remembered, and socialization reversed. The tyranny of the status quo is temporarily broken. Telling one's story is immediately empowering since it puts every student in the role of teacher as he or she brings to the surface the emotional subtext of his or her political philosophy.

SOCRATIC CIRCLE—COMBINING THE SEARCH FOR DEMOCRACY AND ENLIGHTENMENT

Socratic discussion presupposes at least two conditions: (1) a shared concern for "the good of all"—the improvement of the human condition through the pursuit of knowledge, and (2) recognition that the "all" of our community are unique others—moral agents who constitute part of the problem and solution for each of us in our personal search for the "best life possible together." Each discussant needs to understand that everyone's honest opinion carries some relevant truth. In particular, one can often learn most from those with whom one radically disagrees.

Horkheimer clarifies the movement of thought through the Socratic dialectic from individual experience toward intersubjectivity—a shared vision of the whole and, by extension, the good of the whole. He considers the example of the Socratic definition of courage: "When the interlocutor clings to his definition that courage means not running away from the battlefield, he is made to realize that in certain situations, such behavior would not be a virtue but foolhardiness, as when the whole army is retreating and a single individual attempts to win the battle all by himself" (Horkheimer 1972: 265).

Like the philosopher returning to the cave, the contradiction (antithesis) of what is initially given (the thesis) embodies some previously ignored experience. In this example the interlocutor has been obliged to abandon the narrow, conventional definition of "courage" by acknowledging someone else's previously unacknowledged *experience* of a *strategic retreat*. The truth of this thesis, like any thesis, is partial. It needs to be qualified with reference to what it omits, its contradiction, and a more comprehensive formulation. The expanded definition might be something like, "courage is refusing to let fear overwhelm one's duty to the greatest good." The new definition persuades by its greater inclusiveness. It is a work of *synthesis*—a symbolic fusion of the partial truths of thesis and antithesis. Each new thesis is informed by responses to previous theses. In the rapid give and take of face-to-face discussion, it is much more difficult to sustain a mask or keep selfish motives hidden. As the back and forth of discussion is remembered, reflected on, and integrated into an ever expanding, symbolic network of shared experience, it becomes a form of collaborative and living art.

The genius of Socrates was to recognize that this art contained precisely what was increasingly missing in the political life of Athenian democracy. Driving this art is the moral dilemma of Plato's *Republic* and the central problem of the Western political tradition—clarifying one's real needs (the good life) in a political world that recognizes and underwrites only the drive for power and wealth. Like Plato's Athens, we live in a world where the impulses to "goodness, truth, and beauty" are vital but ephemeral.

During his trial, manifestly unafraid of death, Socrates succinctly places this moral sensibility at the center of his "practice and teaching of philosophy." "For I do nothing but go about persuading you all, old and young alike, not to take thought for your persons or your properties, but first and chiefly to care about the greatest improvement of the soul. I tell you that virtue is not given by money, but that from virtue comes money and every other good of man, public as well as private" (Plato 1938:26).

Much of the current talk of "the Socratic method" ignores its moral intention and treats it as a neutral technique to be used indiscriminately in courtroom or classroom.[7] Its truth-generating power depends on the degree of shared concern for all. Understanding the connection between the perfection of my own soul and justice sharpens my attention to the experience of others. As Athenian democracy lost the culture of unselfish concern for the good of the whole, it degenerated into the rule of the lowest common denominator. This possibility remains. When the concern for the whole and the attendant respect for individual "soul work" drives inquiry, the Socratic method becomes a unique, collective art form—what Plato called the "royal art" of building an enlightened and democratic community.

ACTIVE LEARNING STRATEGIES

Explanation and exhortation alone cannot inject the moral content essential to a political and democratic education. It must be built into the structure of the pedagogy and modeled by the instructor. The simple act of spending precious class time on sharing personal stories reinforces the values of reflection and introspection. It models the Socratic example of soul searching and is an appropriate start to any class in which democracy, politics, and active learning are a concern. However, for honest sharing to take place on contentious issues, it is often helpful to periodically remove the teacher from the circle. The reason for this is that there is a spontaneous give-and-take at the heart of deep discussion that the specter of grading can inhibit.

Group Work

One of the simplest ways to facilitate free discussion is to divide the class into workshop groups of approximately five students. If necessary the instructor can leave the classroom until the groups have generated the energy needed for students to start talking from the heart. It is often desirable with students who do not know each other well to appoint a discussion leader whose function is, whenever necessary, but at least once at the beginning and end of the discussion period, to go around the group asking each person by name to give a direct response to the question. After twenty to thirty minutes of group work the class can be reassembled and a spokesperson from each group asked to report to the entire class. The small groups provide safer space for students to get some initial affirmation of their opinions. When the class comes together after such an exercise, there is a marked increase in the number of new voices heard.

Various strategies of group work can take this process further. By role playing, each group is given a different position to develop and justify. This makes it much easier for students who want to disagree with the instructor's perceived position on the issue. For example, in exploring the meaning of the Constitution, one group could collect evidence arguing that the Founding Fathers sacrificed democracy for the sake of creating a capitalist plutocracy. Another group could focus on the emancipatory and democratic aspects of constitution making. A third group might argue that the document was Eurocentric and patriarchal. A fourth group might evaluate the Constitution from the perspective of the spiritual politics of the Confederation of the Iroquois—the Haudenosaunee—which had a considerable influence on the thought of a number of the Founding Fathers.

A further refinement is the jigsaw method. After an initial ten to fifteen minutes of role playing, the students from groups 1, 2, 3, and 4 are reshuffled into four new groups, A, B, C, and D, so that there are representatives of each of the first groups in the new groups. The newly constituted groups then make possible a general sharing of all the arguments and evidence collected during the first role-playing exercise. When students have done the reading, this technique can very efficiently expose the class to most of the evidence for all four positions.

During the sharing process, every student will also have to move between the role of teacher and learner. After sufficient time for such sharing, students go back to their original groups and attempt an overall synthesis and evaluation. After another fifteen to twenty minutes, the groups share their original positions and their new evaluation with the class and instructor as a whole. It is at this point that the instructor must struggle to orchestrate a general discussion, facilitate an overall synthesis, and conduct an evaluation of all that has transpired. When this method works, the concluding discussion has many more participants expressing a greater range of positions than would be the case without the group work. At the same time, because of the intense interaction and the imaginative effort required to express contrary positions, the possibility of changing minds toward a consensus is much greater. The same dynamic that worked in Athens to build a responsible political culture generates the more persuasive synthesis.

Time to Think

Thinking, reflection, introspection, and contemplation need to be built into the course and class time as part of disciplined inquiry. The problem with the teaching of thinking is that it can go on for years about a single issue without producing what is often the bottom line for administrators—

a "measurable outcome." While invisible to the spectator, thinking is the most underrated and ignored practice in higher education. Yet considerable thought is required for the higher-order cognitive functions of synthesis and evaluation. Connections—relating the part to the whole, the political to the personal and so forth—tend to appear after long, concentrated reflection on a mass of detail. Suddenly the gestalt gels into an "aha!" experience. The more challenging the material, the more time is needed.

For example, when the high school version of Columbus' discovery meets the new multicultural scholarship, many students are stunned and confused. They need time to rethink European-American history from an indigenous perspective in order to understand what Russell Means might be referring to when he said on the occasion of the Columbus quintcentennial that "Christopher Columbus makes Hitler look like a juvenile delinquent."

Most students are overwhelmed by the quantity of required reading and memorization. To ensure that the class is adequately prepared for discussion, I carefully distinguish between an essential minimum and recommended readings—sometimes even specifying pages. In addition, I encourage students to leave themselves enough time to reflect on what they have read rather than simply skimming great quantities. Often, more intellectual mileage can be gained by deep reflection on a controversial thesis than by rushing to cover superficially all points of view.

Direct Questioning

It is important to remember that forced disclosures from a reluctant student can backfire by intimidating the rest of the class. I find bright and knowledgeable students sometimes become tongue-tied when put on the spot. To avoid this adversarial atmosphere, which tends to work against deep reflection, I explain that direct questions are "invitations to participate." If students need more time to think or clarify their feelings or simply feel unwilling to expose themselves on a particular issue at a particular time, they can decline such invitations without penalty. Rather than "letting students off the hook," I've found such a permissive approach increases spontaneous participation in discussion and active involvement. End-of-term student evaluations consistently give my classes a maximum or close to the maximum rating in terms of fostering an environment conducive to discussion, questioning, and participation in general. One talks best when one talks from the heart. This cannot be dictated from the outside.

THE DIALECTIC OF EVALUATION

A few reckless proponents of a democratic pedagogy give up attempts to grade their students. Seeing all power differentials as inherently oppressive and antidemocratic, they allow students to choose their own course content, set their own exams, and grade themselves. Hidden in this relic of unreflective, sixties' radicalism is a deep cynicism that flies in the face of common sense: a belief that power can never serve the good of all and that all opinions are equally worthwhile. Such a notion also violates the deep democracy implicit in the Socratic practice of philosophy. Recognizing that every perspective has some value is not the same as valuing every contribution equally.

Interestingly, some research shows that students regard such indiscriminate generosity as unfair. Rita Rodabaugh, director of the Academy for the Art of Teaching at Florida International University, points out that at one institution, while 74 percent of faculty ranked themselves 1 or 2 on a scale of 10 where 1 represented most fair, only 12 percent of students at the same institution ranked their professors as fair. Research indicates that students rate as unfair professors who let students choose their own course content, create their own exams, or grade themselves (Rodabaugh 1994). Students quite reasonably expect the professor to have some expertise, prioritize the knowledge to be acquired by students, and give criteria for satisfactory completion of the course.

The discipline of the Socratic method can provide criteria for distinguishing minimal satisfactory performance (say a grade of C) from very good (B) and excellent (A). While evidence of having done the reading, attending class, and completing written assignments in most cases will ensure at least a C, signs of the higher-order cognitive functions—critical reflection, evaluation, and synthesis of multiple and opposing perspectives—qualify for a B or A grade. Since these higher-order functions tend to be "on" or "off," they provide relatively unambiguous criteria for distinguishing a B from a C. Signs of critical self-reflection include a willingness to reflect on one's initial position by listening to opposing viewpoints and then attempting to integrate them with one's starting point. In written papers this involves the attempt to join the issue. For example, in defending the Founding Fathers as democratic one needs to deal with James Madison's critique of direct democracy in Federalist Paper 10.

Throughout the course, I stress synthesis as a necessary complement to analysis. Synthesis is the process by which the trajectory of the discussion is remembered and the truth content in the various twists and turns is integrated into a shared understanding. One way of developing this faculty is to require term papers to synthesize as well as analyze. One just has to reflect on how many essay questions begin with "analyze" to realize how neglected "synthesis" is. The final paper asks for an integration of several shorter papers written throughout the semester. This accomplishes two things: (1) it sets up writing as a form of inquiry and (2) it emphasizes the importance of rewriting as an aspect of good writing.

Thoughtful writing complements class discussion by focusing reflection on large bodies of material for extended periods. Such contemplation tends to generate meaningful connections between previously isolated bits of information. Reflecting at the end of the semester on material covered from the beginning tends to lead to deeper insights that stay with a student after the course is over.

For example, I begin the course by evaluating Columbus' achievement from a variety of European and Indian perspectives. By the end of the course students have a much deeper understanding of the larger significance of the incipient global capitalism Columbus represented. At the same time, they also have a more detailed appreciation for Native American civilization after the class has considered the contribution of the League of the Iroquois to American democracy. By the end of the semester Columbus gets a far more differentiated and balanced evaluation, that is, a synthesis.

Intention, attitude, and motivation are important components of the Socratic method, but the grading of "effort" is problematic. Research indicates that students only regard consideration for effort as fair in the case of borderline grades (Rodabaugh 1994). However, effort need not be rigidly separated from other more substantive educational goals. I have found that when effort is directed toward the Socratic enterprise, many students experience something of a breakthrough into the higher-order cognitive functions. This motivation intensifies when they realize that, independent of grade, the payoff is in quality of life. One anonymous student commented, "I went in (to class) as a fraction of a person and came out a whole individual." The primary requirement is a desire for improving self and society through an ever expanding self-awareness.

Thus, if a standard paper reveals such an expression of self, the instructor will know that great effort has been expended in the process and can give an A not only for effort, but also for a high level of synthesis, both intellectually and personally.

Of course, as noted above, in a true Socratic dialogue, the teacher—as coequal learner—should also be open to evaluation by the students. From time to time I hear skepticism, particularly from administrators, concerning the validity and reliability of student evaluations of instruction. Yet convincing research on reliability goes back to Herman Remmers in 1927 and has been reaffirmed by recent work. There seems to be a consensus that: (1) student judgments generally agree with those of administrators and teaching colleagues, (2) students do not change their minds after they have been out of college for a few years, and (3) when several teachers teach sections of the same course, students of the higher-rated instructor score higher on standard achievement tests.

It makes sense, does it not, that in matters of increased interest and motivation there are few better measures of outcome than the student's own perception (McKeachie 1990). What has been perhaps the greatest help in my developing a democratic and empowering pedagogy has been the growing number of student evaluations referring to the Socratic method.

THE "QUALITY CIRCLE"—TEACHERS LEARNING AND STUDENTS TEACHING

At the beginning of the semester a group of five or so student representatives is elected from a class of about twenty-five, with suggestions from the instructor, where necessary, to ensure a representative group of students. Their job is to look critically at the class and solicit evaluations from other class members. They then discuss what they have gleaned at regular meetings with me without revealing the identity of their source. Since there is no reason for the meetings to be private, any student may show up for any meeting to participate or to simply observe. Should the entire class turn up the protection of anonymity would be lost but this has never been a problem.

The discussions in the circle are often frank and passionate. It is particularly important, therefore, to thank the group periodically for feedback. Many teachers have a hard time with this, especially at first, and with listening carefully to whatever comes up. After a little testing, I start receiving some remarkably penetrating criticisms and suggestions covering every aspect of the course, from my accent and the quality of my blackboard handwriting to content and all the techniques discussed above.

Since the members of the circle do not have to own their comments, there are few penalties for honest criticism. As the class gains experience with the lessons of the Socratic method and the medicine wheel, it becomes quite evident why I benefit from honest responses—no matter how critical. To reinforce this I make a point of responding to relevant and useful suggestions. It is interesting how many students interpret this as a sign that I really care about them. One student wrote: "He met with the quality circle volunteers after every class. This showed me . . . that he cared about his students. He consistently wanted to know [the] opinion of the circle, if there was feedback. Then he applied what feedback he received. I hope he sustains this style. It would be a shame if he ignores what he did this summer. I am privileged to have him."

In one of my recent upper-division political science classes, eight out of the twenty-one students gave comparably positive responses mentioning my use of the quality circle as contributing to the success of the class. None of the responses were negative. Of all the techniques associated with active learning, this is the one that is most often credited with improving teacher satisfaction. It is also probably the most effective single technique for increasing honest student participation in all aspects of class. I believe the reason for its success is that despite its recent associations with the blitzkrieg of Japanese business, it institutionalizes deep dimensions of the Socratic epistemology.[8]

The primary function of the circle is to provide the instructor with immediate and honest student feedback. One doesn't have to wait until end-of-semester evaluations, when it is too late, to find out where the course failed. As the instructor responds to the give-and-take of discussion in the circle, a continual fine tuning of all aspects of the course becomes possible, and is particularly useful for beginning instructors and those prone to neurotic postmortems of each class. Some problems actually turn out to be imaginary and real ones are immediately identified. Corrective measures can be taken and the overachieving teacher can sleep easily at night. Students are empowered by my visibly acting in accordance with my Socratic convictions—that no one has all the answers and everyone benefits from a more fearless and honest discourse. As one student wrote, "I liked his idea of a quality circle in getting feedback from students so that he can learn and improve himself as well as improving the course. Shows tremendous character and honesty in being vulnerable. I felt valued as a student because he made me feel that I, too, had an important opinion."

Regular use of such a strategy speeds a subtle but profound transformation of class culture. The students in the circle are put in the position of *apprentice* instructors, not equals, being required to think about the class as a whole from my perspective. They teach me the student perspective while I share with them my teaching experience and my vision of an ideal class. The collaborative approach encourages them to take responsibility. The reflective depth, looking at the class from my point of view, stimulates their interest, attentiveness, and participation, and has a ripple effect on other students in the class. Class discussion becomes more focused and passionate as everyone begins to realize they are part of a collaborative teaching-learning enterprise.

TEACHING AS RESEARCH—THE ART OF POLITICAL TRANSFORMATION

Before I revised my manuscript for this chapter, I called a number of graduates who had taken several of my classes to see what stayed with them once they were out of school, in the "real world." The first student stressed how my classes opened her up to a "new kind of politics . . . politics tied to community building," adding that she particulary appreciated the community spirit of my classes. She told me that she now understood politics as "an ongoing project connected to lifelong learning." Another student told me that he particularly valued understanding the connection between philosophical inquiry, soul-searching, and "practical values" or "new possibilities in politics."

A third student informed me that he really valued "the philosophical approach—the examined life—as being fundamental to creating the just society." According to him no other class succeeded as much in developing the students' ability to think critically. He also appreciated the way in which the use of discussion and the quality circle "gave the students the feeling that they have worth and that their opinions really matter." He concluded, "the very fact that you are coming to me now and asking me for my evaluation is a demonstration of what I mean."

A fourth former student found that she had integrated the Socratic method into her daily life. It provided a framework for her in reading the paper, understanding current affairs, and talking to people. Again I heard an appreciation for "the emphasis on theory—the connection of foundational, philosophical thinking to practical issues." She also liked the way "the classes stressed a two-way process between professor and student." This, she added, "changed the classroom dynamics . . . making the classroom a safer place for students to express themselves."

Of course not all my student evaluations are so unreservedly positive. I get regular complaints about too much material from one or two students in every class. The method is hardly infallible. Occasionally students notice that I do have opinions on everything, although I hold back on strident declarations of my own position on specific issues since, for me, the central normative issue is the Socratic method. However, the occasional student still feels inhibited as did this one: "At times I thought his views were biased toward a subject instead of being neutral, which made me feel uncomfortable in responding to the discussions. I didn't want to go against his views."

As I have gained encouragement from student feedback over the years and as I have explored alternative pedagogies, I find myself visualizing the entire course as a work of political art. I am the conductor of the orchestra. My medium is a composite of class time, student attention and activity, lecture content style and length, discussion, role playing, student testimony, guest speakers, in-class writing exercises, and, finally, the strategic use of hard-hitting film, art, and music. My goal is to craft these components so that they move students, and myself, through a collective, transformative experience toward a growing, shared vision of the good of the whole. Since my medium has a mind of its own, the creative autonomy of my students was a precondition for success, and my control, in principle, is limited. Success, while dependent on my leadership, becomes more a matter of collective creativity—the transformation of a college class into more of a philosophical and democratic community.

Such a vision of teaching politics can help heal the deep cleavage between research and teaching. The classroom provides a laboratory for the most ambitious intellectual synthesis—building linguistic and personal bridges of understanding between the philosopher and the citizen. At the same time, both are transformed into members of a community. Whatever mix of altruism or callow opportunism students bring to class, they are for better or worse part of the political reality the philosopher has to communicate with and understand. Teaching can be a way for political thinkers to explore and help transform the lifeworld of their student-citizens, transforming themselves in the process. Without such a democratically based value commitment, pedagogic techniques remain confined to the realm of manipulation and politics as usual.

NOTES

1. "This then, which gives to the objects of knowledge their truth and to him who knows them his power of knowing, is the Form or essential nature of Goodness" Francis Cornford, trans., *Plato's Republic* (New York: Oxford University Press, 1972), p. 215.

2. Paulo Freire, *Pedagogy of the Oppressed* (New York: Continuum Publishing Co., 1970).

3. For a good introduction to and evaluation of the research on teaching since World War I see Wilbert McKeachie of the National Center for Research to Improve Postsecondary Teaching and Learning, University of Michigan, "Research on College Teaching: The Historical Background," *Journal of Educational Psychology* 82, no. 2 (1990): 189–200. For a readable digest of recent literature on active learning see Charles Bonwell and James A. Eison, *Active Learning: Creating Excitement in the Classroom*, ASHE-ERIC Higher Education Report, No. 1 (Washington, D.C.: 1991).

4. The notion of a multicivilizational truth quest that gives birth to history and then orders human society is at the core of Eric Voegelin's philosophy of history. See Eric Voegelin, *Order and History*, 5 vols. (Baton Rouge: Louisiana State University Press, 1959–87). For the crystallization of his philosophical thought see vol. 5 in particular.

5. C.G. Jung reformulates much of this shamanic wisdom in the categories of depth psychology. For a major contribution to an ethical and political implication of Jungian depth psychology see Erich Neumann, *Depth Psychology and a New Ethic* (New York: Putnam, 1969).

6. For a rather turgid philosophical meditation on the structure of the story in history see Eric Voegelin, *Order and History*, vol. 5, *In Search of Order* (Baton Rouge: Louisiana State University Press, 1987), p. 24. For poetic attempt to reconstruct contemporary cosmology as a cosmic creation story see the work of Brian Swimme and Thomas Berry, especially Brian Swimme, "The Resurgence of Cosmic Storyteller," *Revision* 9, no. 2 (Winter/Spring 1987), and Brain Swimme and Thomas Berry, *The Universe Story: A Celebration of the Unfolding of the Cosmos from the Primordial Flaring Forth to the Ecozoic Age* (San Francisco: Harper, 1992).

7. See for example James Overholser, "Socrates in the Classroom," *College Teaching* 40, no. 1 and Frank Guillizza III, "In-Class Debating in Public Law Classes as a Complement to the Socratic Method," *PS: Political Science and Politics* 24, no. 4 (December 1991): 703. Even Richard Paul, with his concern for the connection between moral education and critical thinking tends to refer to the Socratic method as a "technique." See *Critical Thinking: What Every Person Needs to Survive in a Rapidly Changing World* (Sonoma, Calif.: Sonoma State University: Center for Critical Thinking, 1990).

8. There has been a rapid growth of interest in applying the principle of total quality management (TQM) to higher education. Since the idea comes out of the

explosion of quality in Japanese industry, most of the literature focuses on "continuous improvement," "quality," and measurement of outcome. The connection between the method and empowerment through a Socratic epistemology so far seems to have been largely ignored. For an introduction to the ideas as applied to higher education, plus extensive bibliography see Ellen Earle Chaffee and Lawrence A. Sherr, *Quality: Transforming Postsecondary Education*, ASHE-ERIC Higher Education Report, No. 3, (Washington D.C.: 1992).

REFERENCES

Barnes, C. P. 1983. "Questioning in College Classrooms." In C. L. Ellner and C. P. Barnes, *Studies of College Teaching*, 61-81. Lexington, Mass.: Lexington Books. Quoted in James Eison, Fred Janzow, and Charles Bonwell, 1990.

Bonwell, Charles and James A. Eison, 1991. *Active Learning: Creating Excitement in the Classroom*. Washington D.C.: ASHE-ERIC Higher Education Report No. 1, 1991.

Eison, James A., Fred Janzow, and Charles Bonwell. 1990. "Active Learning Development Workshops: Or Practicing What We Teach." *The Journal of Staff, Program and Organization Development* 5, no. 2 (Summer).

Horkheimer, Max. 1972. *Critical Theory, The Social Function of Philosophy*. New York: Seabury Press.

———. 1974. *The Eclipse of Reason*. New York: Seabury Press.

Jung, Carl G. 1973. *Mandala Symbolism*. Princeton: Princeton University Press.

Lawry, John D. 1990. "Caritas in the Classroom: The Opening of the American Student's Heart." *College Teaching* 38, no. 3 (Summer): 83-87.

McKeachie, Wilbert. 1990. "Research on College Teaching: The Historical Background." *Journal of Educational Psychology* 82, no. 2: 189-200.

Paul, Richard. 1990. *Critical Thinking: What Every Person Needs to Survive in a Rapidly Changing World*. Sonoma, Calif.: Sonoma State University, Center for Critical Thinking.

Plato. 1938. *Portrait of Socrates, being the Apology, Crito and Phaedo of Plato in an English Translation*. Edited by Richard Livingstone. Oxford: The Clarendon Press.

Rodabaugh, Rita. 1994. "In the Name of the Student." *Teaching Excellence* 6, no. 3.

Rowe, M. B. 1974a. "Pausing Phenomena; Influence on the Quality of Instruction." *Journal of Psycholinguistic Research* 3: 203-224(a). Quoted in James Eison, Fred Janzow, and Charles Bonwell, 1990.

Rowe, M. B. 1974b. "Wait-time and Rewards as Instructional Variables." *Journal of Research in Science Teaching* 11: 81-94. Quoted in James Eison, Fred Janzow, and Charles Bonwell, 1990.

Storm, Hyemeyohsts. 1972. *Seven Arrows*. New York: Harper and Row.

Vlastos, Gregory. 1991. *Socrates: Ironist and Moral Philosopher*. Ithaca, N.Y.: Cornell University Press.

PART II

Beyond Classrooms and Internships

A group of criminal justice majors are placed in a wide array of law enforcement agencies to work for the duration of a summer. At the end of their stints, they attend a special seminar where they present oral reports on their experiences. Each intern details the chores she or he performed in the workplace—at a field FBI office, with a county sheriff, at a small-town police department, at ATF headquarters in Washington, D.C. How did their days go? What was the patrol routine? How up-to-date was the ballistics lab? What did they learn about "policing?"

This scenario portrays one type, if not the predominant model, of college-level experiential education programs in the classic rendition of technical education. Students applied some of the knowledge passed on to them in the classroom while working in a real-world situation. They then relay their hands-on experiences back to the instructor and one another. Is there anything wrong with this picture?

If the American college educational experience is supposed to prepare students for the workplace, to be a higher-level vo-cational training, then nothing would be amiss in the above depiction of an actual course in a major state university in the 1990s. However, if the liberal arts, higher educational mission also includes the goal of training citizens to be better citizens—not only better police, public administrators, business persons, legislators and/or social workers—then such experiential education, that is, purely technical internships, are not an answer to this goal. Something else must be involved. Experiential education, as discussed in Part I, must be something more than a practical introduction to labor and market conditions.

Let's face some harsh facts about the times in which we live. Modern college students are keenly aware of the increasing difficulties in obtaining a well-paying, secure position once they conclude their college careers. Why shouldn't they be? The future of work in "the global marketplace" is shaky. Modern college educations are expensive propositions, leaving many students deeply in debt. What will be the payoff for such a heavy investment if not a good job?

Thus, it is hardly surprising that savvy students see internships as a smart way to make contacts that will help them land some kind of personally rewarding, permanent employment in the future. They see prestigious internships as showy entries on their resumes. Indeed, some of the more centrally located, prestigious citadels of higher education in America proudly announce internships as major attractions. Georgetown University, in its 1995 Summer internship brochure, proclaims that

Students decide to attend our Summer Institutes for a variety of reasons—to have the chance to live in our nation's capital during the Summer, to experience the rigor of Georgetown University, to have a memorable and valuable internship in Washington, or to make contacts among Washington's power elite. Students quickly realize that one of the greatest benefits of the institute experience is the network of contacts that they make. It's not up to the student to see any bigger picture. It's up to the professor and the college to paint the whole portrait.

As we noted in our introductory essay, a good deal of thought has already been given to this matter and there have been a number of successful approaches that go beyond internship and mere "on-the-job training" experiential learning. So what is added to the vocational features?

For one thing, there is *critical* theory. The idea here is to get the students to think analytically about the social, economic and political circumstances under which they toil in the internship by arming them with theory that harbors perspectives contrary to conventional wisdom. For another, there is *reflection*. This yields some time for students to bounce their experiences off the theory and deliberate on how they are affected personally. And finally, there is the opportunity to consider *alternatives*, how the future can be different for themselves and for all citizens who cry out for a meaningful say in what can be a better life. All of this, added to the technical training, makes the experiential education an experience in democratic learning.

The following two chapters describe the emerging field of

service learning or public service learning. The authors, leaders in the emerging field, relate the theory behind their efforts to link a democratically oriented theory and curriculum to a democratic, experiential education process. They also explain what they learned from and about students who traveled a road of education beyond internships.

3

Service Learning: Integrating Community Issues and the Curriculum

Richard A. Couto

The current emphasis on service learning offers students and faculty a common vehicle to integrate social and political issues into the curriculum. Some of the roots of the current emphasis on service learning go back to the democratic movements of the 1960s and 1970s, especially the student movement. Ironically, a decade after the students voiced their demands for change and relevance, college and university administrators voiced their support for community service. This chapter explains some background of service learning and how its many forms may improve the teaching of democracy.

THE STUDENT MOVEMENT, SERVICE LEARNING, AND HIGHER EDUCATION

I came to service learning from the student movement of the 1960s. My graduate studies at the University of Kentucky were punctuated with demonstrations against the war in Vietnam, strip-mining in Eastern Kentucky, and Appalachian poverty. Never, even in my wildest delusion of political efficacy, did I believe that these actions were internships. Yet I knew they offered profound lessons that prompted serious and sometimes angry classroom discussions. The discussions sometimes became demands for new programs and courses and for new forms of representation and participation for students in decision making. Many of these demands met serious opposition. According to some teachers, administrators, and state officials, the demand that the university end its academic isolation and admit and revise its role as a social institution meant the ruin of teaching and research. Or, in the more colorful analogies of the time, that the inmates had taken over the asylum.

Some faculty members heard the demands for relevance and involvement only as an interruption of their work. In one particular, critical incident, now a technique in which I train my students, a prestigious, that is, well-published, faculty member came storming out of his office complaining of the noise. Students in the plaza sixteen stories below were chanting slogans that advocated a halt to the bombing in Cambodia. On the stairwell leading to the eighteenth-floor boardroom, students were attempting, with little success, to enter the meeting of the board and to have its members sign a statement opposing the expansion of the war. They spilled out into the hallways of the political science department. The faculty member approached the elevator with his own loud protest, "I'm going home. I can't get any work done here." The secretary of the political science department looked at him and chided, "You're not going anywhere. If you don't stay and make sense of what's going on here, who's supposed to?" Well, he left anyway. As far I know, he kept going, traveling further into a subfield of specialization of political socialization and into the apparatus of the university that supported this form of scholarly work untouched by the Vietnam War except for its role in generating hypotheses.

Fortunately for me, a few faculty members reacted quite differently to the social movements, including those of students, around them. My efforts to find a "safe" dissertation topic far removed from my original intent to look at the politics of Appalachian poverty ran into the stubborn resistance of a persuasive faculty member, despite the fact that he had just been denied tenure. I explained to him that the department had thwarted every plan I had to study the politics of poverty, but he would not let me off the hook. He reminded me that I chose the University of Kentucky in order to do just that type of study. Every time I explained that no one was doing what I wanted to do, he countered, "Then you should start. Especially if it is important like you say it is." I did as he suggested. Eventually, faculty in other departments offered new courses on social issues and brought in speakers with direct connection to them as instructors, and the University of Kentucky began an Appalachian Center. Students and faculty had made change.

In 1975, when I went to Vanderbilt University to direct the Center for Health Services, I thought of the center as a remnant of the preceding decade and the resulting efforts at social change on college campuses. Student projects of the center, such as the Appalachian Student Health Coalition, conducted community services as tools to support local leaders in their organizing and development efforts. By 1980, the various projects had assisted local leaders in the development of more than twenty community-directed primary care centers in rural areas without health services and in the establishment of citizens groups such as Save Our Cumberland Mountains, which is still going strong after twenty-five years. Students, with a few key faculty allies and modest university support, were making change.

I learned many valuable lessons in those first few years (Couto 1982). Our work seldom started any actual organizing; instead more often it renewed the union or civil rights organizing that had preceded it. I learned the problems of running a program of social change and democratic development from a university base, which are spelled out in Part III. Here I will focus on the lessons learned about students, their development, and their education.

Fundamentally, I learned that the more students felt they were working effectively for positive social change, the more they reported outcomes associated with liberal arts education and personal development. Ancillary lessons included the importance of orientation, how to distinguish a good learning community context from a poor one, and the importance of reflection. A later section of this chapter discusses these elements of service learning. I also learned that Freedom Summer, the Appalachian Volunteers, and other central events and actors of social movements of just a few years ago offered less and less relevance to students and funders for the work of the student projects as the 1980s began. I learned how quickly the social environment and institutional context for programs can change and the importance of adapting if you want to continue programs of democratic change.

Reports on higher education in the early 1980s expressed the need to reinstate democratic values and civic participation into the curriculum. In contrast with the concern over student activism a decade before, the problem now seemed to be student apathy (Levine 1980). Because of Vanderbilt's Center for Health Services' reputation, the chancellor was invited to the formative meetings of Campus Compact. I served on an initial advisory committee and marveled as the dozen or so college and university presidents slowly shaped this national association. It now has over four hundred members that support community service in higher education.

Based on lessons I had already acquired, I wanted to know why these presidents had decided to take action. What preceded it? What was it renewing? I learned that many of these presidents had been middle-level administrators during the activism of the 1960s and 1970s. They had learned lessons about the social role of educational institutions and the value of social involvements and commitments of students for the educational mission of their institutions. Howard Swearer, president of Brown University in the 1980s, recalled for me his role as a faculty member in a training program for the first set of Peace Corps volunteers. Twenty years later he recalled the gleam in the eyes of those first volunteers and he wanted to see it again—thus his pivotal role in Campus Compact. Despite their commitment, however, the presidents steadfastly refused to bring their endorsement of community service to the faculty of their schools or to attempt to integrate community service and the curriculum. Evidently, some faculty still found the essence of academia some distance from social issues and problems, and the presidents feared it would take too much political capital to approach the curriculum.

Soon, however, college administrators and public officials found themselves running to catch up with numerous student initiatives on community service. By the 1990s, as we explained in the Introduction, community service had found a place on campus, but only at the margin. A genuine institutionalization of community service required incorporation into the core educational mission of colleges and universities, the curriculum, and that was as rare as a liberal at a Republican convention. In addition, after almost a decade of experience, it had become quite apparent that community service, per se, was neither a pedagogy nor democratic.

Without structured and informed reflection on the political implications of *student* service and the related issues of inequality and power—some movement analysis—human needs in community service could metamorphose into "feel good" efforts that conveyed many false impressions to students. I listened with dismay to accounts of the value of community service as students explained how they had helped solve a complex, social problem in a week-long volunteer effort; how they had brought hope to the lives of children with severe social and economic problems through an afternoon outing with them; or how they had paid for their social and economic advantage by serving a short stint in a soup kitchen. The elements of truth in these statements innocently disregard the significance of the issues. Eventually, others had dismay as well. Educators and administrators turned to what some call "service learning," a synthesis of community service and course work that gives students relevant data and theory for reflective problem solving. The work of the National Society for Experiential Education stimulated some of this development and the work of others to articulate and document the theory and practice of service learning. The democratic changes of the student movement entered a new phase of its long march through the institutions.

A DEFINITION OF SERVICE LEARNING

Service learning is not just community service, experiential education, or classroom instruction, but rather all three and more—combining all of them synergistically when done correctly. Community service alone, as important as it is, omits the deliberate and intentional *learning* of service learning. It provides the text of service learning, but like any other course text, its explication and elaboration depends on structured, analytical reflection and discussion in a classroom. Obviously, service learning exceeds classroom instruction because it requires that students acquire specific experiences—

real-life events unavailable in the classroom—upon which to reflect. Service learning prescribes experiences and then studies them in the classroom. The assigned service is rooted in a real social need with political origins, and thus is one particular form of experiential education.

By way of definition then, service learning is an out-of-classroom learning activity, like an internship, that has planned and explicit learning objectives, such as classroom instruction. It has intended benefits for both the students and those served. Ideally, people on campus and in the community cooperate to facilitate and direct learning that is embedded in the services that the students provide, with the students accountable to those served. The services provided are intended to create a positive change in the lives of the people served including a reduced need for the provided services.

This emphasis on community service within the public and nonprofit sector toward an improved future differentiates service learning from legislative internships or those in administrative offices of government. While service learning offers insight into politics apart from government, there is a risk that community service becomes a surrogate for politics and public service. One part of the tradition of voluntary associations, dating back to de Tocqueville, emphasizes voluntary action as a substitute for politics and government. At the very least, service learning should make students aware of the political nature of this tradition. At its best, service learning should transform community service into public service by tracing social needs and responses to their political origins.

On the educational side, service learning, when done properly, infuses the humanist traditions of higher education with the call of the progressive tradition for democratic practice and reform. For example, David Winter (1981) and his colleagues examined the "sacred texts" of the humanist tradition, expressed by the liberal arts, from Plato to various recent educational commissions. They assembled the canons of faith in the humanist tradition of education listed in Table 3.1. John Duley, a practitioner of reflective experiential education within the progressive tradition, carefully enumerated the canons of faith of experiential education. These are also listed in Table 3.1 and compared with the canons of the humanist tradition. The emphasis on critical thinking and putting theory to practice within these faiths provides some educators hope that humanist education and progressive education are *liberating* and not merely liberal arts. Zelda Gamson (1984), for example, argues that liberating education facilitates students' critical awareness of the forces that have shaped their lives, of the power they have to make things different, and of the choices they have about exercising their power. Such aspirations echo the emphasis on experimentation in the work of John Dewey and on praxis in Paulo Freire's work.

Service learning relates national service to education as well. William James provided a very early formulation of goals and values of community or national service for American youth. Indeed, self-sacrifice for the public

Table 3.1
Comparison of the Goals of Service Learning with the Goals of Liberal
Arts Education, Experiential Education, and National Service

SERVICE LEARNING	LIBERAL ARTS EDUCATION (Humanist Tradition)	EXPERIENTIAL EDUCATION (Progressive Tradition)	NATIONAL SERVICE
Critical Thinking	Critical Thinking	Putting Theory into Practice	
Expanding Learning Styles	Learning to Learn	Learning to Learn Independently; Acquiring Knowledge; and Research and Analysis	
Human Development	Independence in Thinking Self-Assurance and Leadership Self-Control and Broader Loyalties	Increased Personal Growth and Development; Self-Confidence; Understanding; and Reliance	Human Development
Personal Values and Interpersonal Skills	Egalitarian, Liberal Values Empathy Mature Socio-emotional judgment	Becoming a Responsible Citizen; Acquiring and Developing Specific Skills; Problem Solving; Interpersonal and Group Process Skills	Experience in Altruism Social Integration
Career Exploration		Exploring Careers	Career Exploration
New Cultural Appreciation	Participating in and Enjoying Cultural Experiences		

interest forms an essential element of national service. Other elements in the canons of national service are listed in Table 3.1 and compared with those of the other educational traditions we have touched upon.

Combining these traditions permits us to clearly relate the goals of service learning to other, more familiar elements of higher education and citizen development. Table 3.1 lists the goals of service learning in the left-hand column and the elements of the other traditions in the three right-hand columns. While service learning is not a democratic pedagogy in itself, its goals of (1) critical thinking; (2) accommodating varied learning styles; (3) fostering human development; (4) improving interpersonal skills and clarification of personal values; and (5) appreciation for culture, provide a solid foundation for democratic teaching and practice. Moreover, by its bond to academia, service learning provides ample space from which to push the relatively rigid boundaries of educational institutions in the direction of improved democratic practice.

SERVICE LEARNING AND TEACHING DEMOCRACY

To achieve its goals, service learning, like any mode of teaching, has to incorporate principles of effective practice. At least two sets of principles have evolved from the practice of service learning. In 1989, at a conference conducted at the Wingspread conference center by the Johnson Foundation of Racine, Wisconsin, a group of educators articulated ten principles for the effective practice of service learning (Honnet and Poulsen 1989). Independently, Benjamin Barber (1992) conducted university-wide discussions at Rutgers that eventually articulated nine governing principles of service learning that linked community service to civic education. This chapter will examine three components of those principles: the community context, orientation, and reflection.

The Community Context: Choosing the Right Material with Which to Build

Teaching democracy through service learning requires at least two things: appraising the community context in which the service learning takes place—a community of need—and collaboration with a community of response. The community context of service learning should raise explicit questions about power and inequality, something that other "internships" rarely do. It will do this, however, only if the instructor is deliberate in the selection of the service the students will conduct (Couto 1990). Service should involve a problem that groups are organized to do something about, like breast cancer or rezoning. The service should also involve issues of representation and participation in the political process, apart from the polling booth, that exemplify the use of power in its different dimensions (Gaventa 1980:3-32).

An appropriate site for service learning includes not only the need of a particular community but the ability and willingness of local residents to act on that need. Community assessment therefore requires that teacher-facilitators of service learning programs investigate each site for at least those two groups: the community of need and the community of response.

We generally have a fair sense of various communities of need, although we tend to lump them into large, undifferentiated categories that tell us little about the root cause of their needs: the poor, the homeless, the sick, the imprisoned, and so forth. On the other hand, we may have some cognition of the broader issues that beset various communities of need: unemployment, strip-mining, pollution, hunger, illiteracy, and so on.

We generally lack detailed knowledge about the community of response within a community of need at the beginning of a service learning course or program. The community of response may be as informal as a group of local residents (members of local churches or store owners) who other community residents look to for advice and action in most circumstances and needs. Group response may vary in effectiveness from issue to issue and from community to community.

Local leaders' responses to community needs do not begin with the arrival of outsiders such as service learners or other groups. If one keeps in mind that service learning is not the beginning of community response to some defined need, then one recognizes a service learning program's own need to determine what has preceded it. This not only prepares one better to build on what has gone before, but it also provides a much more certain foundation upon which to build. The history of the community of response may be one of the issues addressed, including personal development of individual members, group and infrastructure development, and other wonderful accomplishments. But it may also have a tradition of issues abandoned due to organizational infighting or to the repeated failure to improve local conditions. If a service learning program takes democratic change seriously, it needs to grasp the problems and prospects of democracy within "helping organizations" and among community leaders with whom it works.

There is also a community of response from outside the community of need. It may be a varied set of voluntary associations and community organizations that depend for their staff and funding on resources outside of the community of need. A storefront ministry to the homeless is an example. These associations and organizations are generally private and nonprofit. They generally have more financial and material resources than the informal leaders within the community of response, although this is not to say that their coffers runneth over or that their resources are adequate. There may be private, profit-making service groups within the community of response as well, such as physicians and health centers. Finally, public agencies are another set of members in the community of response. They have a man-dated and publicly financed role to respond to a community of need. Public health departments and some literacy campaigns are public members of the community of response.

Due to the abundance of need and the scarcity of resources, there is a surplus of politics to grasp and to deal with. Students in service learning generally ignore or do not understand the multilayered, complex phenom-enon of the politics of help and the fit of their own efforts into this form of political life. This includes, of course, understanding that most student service learners are part of a community of response from outside the com-munity of need and generally align themselves with other members of the outside communities of response as their sponsors. Invariably, their college's role and responsibility as a member of the community of response presents an important and legitimate dilemma concerning reflection, deliberation, and political action—but it is a difficult one to comprehend and solve. How much effort and how many resources are colleges actually willing to lend to community change efforts? How safe does a community effort have to be for university participation? How does one work within the university to address a community problem, such as neighborhood development, of which the university may be a part?

The political nature of community service will vary widely depending on how the community sponsor understands the service to the local group. Does the sponsor see it as a pursuit of justice for, by, or of the people of the community of need; as a form of charity from the external community of response to the community of need; as a service exchanged for a fee; or as an organizational output mandated by some distant government agency? Many different political and educational consequences for service learners flow from these and other varied perceptions of service. An agency that sees itself as a vigorous agent of justice, such as an advocacy group for battered women, is much more likely to come into conflict with established authority than an organization, such as a shelter for battered women, that is more concerned with meeting a specified number of open and closed cases that authorities have established as its goal and fund accordingly. Such conflict, or its absence, obviously changes the political nature of the service learning program. Most often helping organizations balance their pursuits of justice and the efficient expenditure of public funds in a political juggling act that students need to learn from and understand.

On a more pragmatic level, the internal environment of an organization teaches a great deal. Institutional environments provide service learners dif-fering environs in regard to closeness of supervision, variety of roles, and insight into office politics. Moreover, the longer the local group or or-ganization has been in existence and the more resources it has, the more likely the group will be accustomed to having student assistance. This often means an established group is more likely to have routinized dealings with students coming in for a brief time. On the other hand, newly formed groups are far less likely to have well-defined roles for service learners and are more inclined to treat them as one of the group, extending greater autonomy to them.

The size and nature of an organization's staff is important, too. Whether a staff is full-time or part-time and paid or voluntary changes the character of an organization. An organization with a full-time, paid staff is more likely to have specific goals and a hierarchical structure with a division of labor than an organization with a part-time, voluntary staff. This distinction will influence the amount and quality of supervision available to and over service learners, the degree of responsibility provided them, and the specific or bureaucratic nature of the roles and tasks assigned to them. A part-time, voluntary staff that understands the organization as pursuing some form of justice for its members—to halt a pollution problem, for example—is more likely to give service learners a great deal of minimally supervised responsibility. This situation may be more difficult for the neophyte service learners than that found in a large, hierarchical organization, such as a public health department, where the supervision tends to be very explicit and the responsibility more likely to be "busy work." Clear, consistent, and capable supervision provides a cornerstone for effective service learning and only an assessment of the community context can determine if such supervision is available.

Obviously then, evaluating a site for service learning extends far beyond determining the need of a community. It must also take account of the political goals of an agency, its capacity to respond to community need, and how it can and/or will treat the students.

In addition to these broad and deeply political issues, service learning programs need to gain information about and to negotiate what jobs service learners might undertake. These questions focus on finding a specific task that addresses what the community needs and what is within the ability and limits of students to deliver. The generosity of people in the community of response extends to giving service learners what they need and they may promise to provide a chore to service learners to satisfy the students' needs and not the needs of the community. Obviously, the task service learners take on should address a problem in the community and not merely satisfy their need for hands-on experiences. Merely "something" for the students to do undermines the political nature and educational importance of the service. The best measures of appropriate work for students are the amount of effort the community of response has put into the task already and what local leaders will do with the fruit of the students' labor.

Several questions summarize and frame the crucial elements of the community context for service learning and its political nature.

- Are the people from the community of response accountable to members of the community of need in some way?
- Do their services have a board of directors, advisors, and so forth?
- Who are the people on the board? Who selects them? To whom are they account-able?
- How are decisions made within the organization? Is it a direct democratic process with full participation and direct representation of the people affected, some form of representative democratic process, or is it autocratic and unresponsive to anyone below?
- Are representatives of the community of need represented on the board as decision makers?
- Do representatives of the community of need participate formally and informally in the internal decision making of the organization?
- Have the services of the agency reached *all* sectors of the community of need?
- Are some residents of the community of need ignored or unserved? Why?

Another set of questions deals with the ability of those in the community of response to mobilize resources within and outside of the community for existing or new services.

- Is there an effort to have local residents provide for their own services even if the effort is limited? If so, what is it? How effective is it? If ineffective, why is it so?
- Are the people in the community of need trained for new roles in the organization through provided or promised services?
- Does the organization foster new links of local residents and outside resources or does the staff control them exclusively? Is the agency creating a culture of depend-ency?
- Can the organization's staff and members continue the work that service learners may start?

These questions do not seek any true or false, correct or incorrect, or other dichotomous resolution. They do not permit us to select the best community context or political setting. However, they will serve as a starting point for what we must do, as educators, to structure reflection, supervision, and analysis in order to understand the political nature of community service and to relate it to a political process of socioeconomic change.

Orientation: Laying the Foundation for Service Learning

Orientation is perhaps the easiest element of service learning pedagogy to underestimate, despite its importance. After all, people in the program are already familiar, and perhaps bored, with the elements of orientation. Nevertheless, orientation provides the best time to share with the service learners the history, goals, and objectives of the program, the background of agencies, and the specific activities of service. In addition, orientation permits the service learners time to get acquainted with one another and their specific roles. This is the time to form the classroom community and to attend to the communal nature of teaching democratically. During this stage, logistical questions such as transportation, payment, reimbursement for expenses, and other administrative matters need to be settled. Furthermore, orientation should start students immediately to think critically, to develop new learning styles, to develop as human beings, to develop interpersonal skills, and to acquire new appreciation for different cultures. In other words, service learning, like other teaching, requires a sound and effective introduction.

The length of the orientation will probably vary with the amount of time that students devote to community service. A Saturday morning stint in home construction with Habitat for Humanity does not require a full-day orientation. An eight-week, full-time, action research project will probably require at least a day of orientation.

Regardless of the time given to it, though, an orientation must include several important elements that prepare students to maximize the knowledge generated by the service. Indeed, it is my view that the orientation phase has to alert students to several changes that will occur in them to one degree or another. First, there is a shift from the dependency they have on faculty to the accountability they should have on their community supervisor and classmates. Second, there is the transposition from a campus culture and its socioeconomic context to the culture and socioeconomic context of a community of need. Third, there is a switch from the acquisition of competence tested in classrooms to the application of competence with consequences for people other than themselves. Finally, there is the movement from a set of tacit assumptions about the community of need to fresh ideas and views based on acquired experience.

An orientation that does not prepare service learners to handle *all* of these shifts, to some degree, will detract both from the quality of learning and the quality of service in their work. A teacher-facilitator can very easily spend the entire duration of a service learning project trying to create some order out of a chaos created from students sorting out the feelings and thoughts inherent in these shifts if they were inadequately prepared. In some cases, the community supervisor will have to assume this task, or at least a part of it. In all cases, an incomplete orientation will reduce the efficiency of the students and the value of the contribution they can make to the community. Moreover, these transitions are important democratic developments since they impart to the students a heightened awareness of accountability and appreciation of socioeconomic contexts of events.

Reflection: Adding Depth and Breadth

Like orientation, the quality of reflection will vary with the time commitment of the service project. A one-half day recreation program with incarcerated youth may not require weekly reflection sessions, but a thirty-hour involvement will require at least that. There are many different formats that can assist reflection. Half-day community service projects might employ a photographer to take slides. The slides can then be processed in a one-hour photo developing shop so that the students can view their morning's work over lunch. Obviously, week-long or semester-long projects permit more opportunities for longer periods of analysis, discussion, self-criticism, systemic critiques, and other elements of reflection.

Journal keeping is another useful tool to provide students with data for these reflection sessions. Journals can also provide faculty with detailed accounts of events and students' reactions to them. There are several excellent guides for constructing journals (Alpert 1987; Hursh 1990; Zimmerman et al. 1990; Stanton and Ali 1982), as most students need plenty of direction and instruction in the art and methods of journal keeping. Teachers may help by asking them to recount specific events or experiences in their journals, or to amplify on critical incidents or events that summarized feelings, thoughts, impressions, and lessons learned. These incidents may include: their first impressions; the clash of expectations with experience; the subtle indications of power relations among men and women, bosses, and staff, and so forth. Obviously, the number and nature of assignments will vary with the nature of the service learning.

The journal supports other methods of fostering reflection. For example, journal entries may be discussed in class and, formally or informally, compared and contrasted with other journal entries. Furthermore, students may be assigned short essays, using their journals to keep notes in preparation for those assignments or as a source for information. One assignment that seems to work well is an essay, "Through the Eyes of Those Served." In this essay, students write a first-person narrative from the viewpoint of a recipient of agency services. This moves students into the life of someone else who then analyzes the setting from an entirely different perspective. This exercise often enhances the students' empathy and social consciousness.

While essays are useful, oral reports bring information back to the whole class that can be used to stimulate class discussion and reflection in a way that compares and contrasts service learning contexts and different individual responses to them. This kind of comparison and contrast also expands and advances the realms of student thought. Moving students beyond simple descriptions of their own personal moods and feelings regarding their experience, the service setting, and the people served permits faculty to evaluate students in terms of their critical and analytical thinking abilities. This also permits faculty to assign grades that distinguish students in terms of how much and how well they have learned. If we are to reach the goals of democratic teaching via service learning, it appears to me that we must get beyond patting everyone on the head for their community service. Instead, we need to transmit serious, systematic, evaluative feedback to students about their abilities to analyze a community setting or service, to assess its significance, to relate and work with people, to deliberate with others, and to apply lessons acquired from one particular setting to another.

Whatever the format and techniques used, reflection should proceed over five phases:

1. Students should *describe* where they were, what they did, what they thought about it, and how they felt. If there are different groups, their descriptions should be compared and contrasted.

2. Students should *compare and contrast* their thoughts and feelings with one another.

3. Based on this information, the group then begins to *analyze* what happened for the group(s) and members. At this point, the political content (including democratic and undemocratic views of service and the need addressed) should emerge clearly. Some people will clearly understand the relationships of power in the context of the service they performed and others will not.

4. Analysis of the events of service and on the individual and group experiences provide the material from which to *generalize*.

5. Once the group has arrived at some generalizations, it discusses how they *apply* to the service they just completed and other activities that they will perform subsequently.

As with any other form of pedagogy, we will want to evaluate the effectiveness of service learning, whatever form it takes. Ultimately, programs of educational institutions will be judged by what and how much students learn, however crude our measures and diverse our definitions of learning. Service learning is no different in this regard since it is part and parcel of the curriculum. Reflection binds service learning to the curriculum.

LINCS: A MODEL OF TEACHING DEMOCRACY BEYOND INTERNSHIPS

I moved to the University of Richmond in 1991 in part because the Jepson School of Leadership Studies was without a curriculum and it sought one that incorporated many of the reforms, including experiential learning and community service, called for in the 1980s. It seemed a place where the integration of community service and the curriculum could happen. Indeed, at the University of Richmond, the Jepson School of Leadership Studies has distributed and nurtured service learning in other schools and departments. Specifically, the Learning in Community Settings (LINCS) Program at the

University of Richmond offers several models for course-related or credit-bearing service learning: (1) community service, (2) school-based instruction, (3) action research, and (4) a community problem-solving (COMPS) seminar. The program thereby offers distinct models of service learning to incorporate into different courses, in different ways. Equally important, this approach implies that political science departments and teachers can disseminate service learning and the teaching of democracy throughout the curriculum, beyond classes in one department.

Community Service

Some instructors require a limited amount of community service, about fifteen hours, to fulfill the requirements for a class or offer students the option of community service in place of another assignment. Russian language students, for example, were assigned Russian émigrés by the Refugee Resettlement Program in Richmond and were expected to meet and talk with those individuals and families, helping them conduct normal activities such as recreation or shopping. In this model, students learned conversational Russian and the émigrés acquired more knowledge of English. Students in special topic courses in political science, for example, AIDS and Public Policy, Women and Politics, or Environmental Politics might be required to work with an agency as a volunteer for twenty hours during the course of the semester.

Though limited, these kinds of experiences can be powerful teaching tools, especially among traditional-aged college students from privileged backgrounds. James MacGregor Burns argues that this group most likely has the least preparation for political leadership in "a pluralized, complex, and open society." Adolescents "in a child-centered affluent suburban community" are likely to have, according to Burns, "linear, monistic, and overwhelmingly cumulative" role demands that lessen their ability "to cope with diversity of persons or roles" (Burns 1978:99).

Service learning has the potential to impact such students immediately and profoundly by illuminating the nature of class and inequality in American life (Couto 1993). In one instance, for example, one University of Richmond student visited a homeless shelter for men and on her first visit reported through her journal, "I was never so aware of my race, my gender, and my socioeconomic class as I was that evening." It was disconcerting for her, if not a little frightening. Her second evening there was "awesome." After her third visit, she volunteered to serve on the board of the agency, representing student volunteers. Her journal entries went on for pages, with deep personal reflection about the site, the men she visited, past and present parental advice, and herself. She now works for a national fraternity coordinating the community service component of their program reform.

Other students may get a blinding flash of the obvious, one that disturbs them. For example, one student claimed, hopefully in a bit of hyperbole, that his trip to his service site, a transitional housing program for homeless women and children, was his first trip off campus other than to go to a bar. During his too brief orientation, eight to ten minutes, the staff member received five phone calls. Three of them were from women looking for a place to stay that night. All of them had to be turned away because the shelter was full. He recalled the impact and his personal confusion over these desperate exchanges: "At this point things began to hit home. Three people and possibly their children will have nowhere to sleep tonight, three. This is America. I go to school with 20 year old people who drive $40,000 cars and there are three families who may have nowhere to sleep in January."

Another student reported learning of three types of community service: "the hands-on, make-the-day-much-easier-than-it-would-have-been-without-me"; the "where you work to make tomorrow better . . . like when you build a house for a homeless family"; and the "white-collar, pass-this-bill-because-it-will-help-a-lot-of-people, excuse-me-while-I-lobby-for-some-earth-shattering-legislation type of community service." His report, thus briefly summarized an implicitly political continuum from apolitical charity to deliberately political advocacy. On a more personal level, he also reported his shock and edification on learning that a mother—who was "bright, intelligent, articulate, attractive, and with-it"—and her six-year-old daughter—who was "energetic, quick, affectionate, artistic, and funny"—had both been addicted to heroin six years before at the birth of the child. This lesson was related to two other lessons he acquired: "every person . . . is special" and "many of the things which I thought would result in the end of the earth [for me] are actually nothing compared to the trials and tribulations some people have endured."

Getting students off campus, into the community for purposes other than visiting a tavern, and into situations in which differences of class and degrees of human need are evident, may be small steps in teaching democracy but surely they are strides in the right direction. The occasional and fragmented political critique, of which we spoke in the Introduction, took on a personal dimension for these students. They understood, in a new sense, that they were part of a society in which expensive automobiles and homelessness traffic side by side. They understood, in a moment, the lessons that *we* as teachers hope will never be lost completely or crowded out by other, *more impersonal* instruction: that social problems touch people who are special and, like everyone else, have the capacity to be affectionate, artistic, and funny. These lessons illustrate two of the five characteristics of democracy that Dewey offered, respect for one another and listening to one another. If democracy and democratic teaching have a common starting point, surely it is the insight that social problems involve both the haves and the have-nots and that members of both groups are human with their foibles and their strengths. This central tenet of popular education is best imparted away from the institutions, including colleges and universities, that spend too much time explaining the merits and functions of inequality and social distinctions. The possibility of teaching the human dimensions of social problems within our institutions offers hope that it is possible to be a democratic teacher in undemocratic settings, a central concern for Paulo Freire.

On a less lofty plane, these examples illustrate how service learning differs from field trips in a significantly political way: students belong in the battered women's shelter, the AIDS project's office, or the public defender's office because they are doing something about the problem, another of Dewey's characteristics of democracy. They are there to learn, but they pay a portion of the debt for their instruction through service. When that service provides students meaningful participation and insight into a public problem, they have reached yet another of Dewey's characteristics of democracy. Students who share the common experience of community service will sometimes build a special and unique camaraderie. Sharing rides to and from the service site brings students together in rudimentary teams. Not only is teamwork and group sharing a welcomed antidote to the ordinary message of individual effort and acquisition of the liberal tradition of education, but it marks yet another characteristic of democracy according to Dewey.

School-Based Service Learning: Community Service and Teaching

The difficulty of finding an adequate site for service learning, one hospitable to a structured opportunity to meet the needs of grade school and high school youth, provides an incentive for school-based service learning. Some instructors offer their students the chance to organize modules of instruction, tutoring, and other forms of teaching. Political socialization classes can take a lively twist with a trip to a nearby high school with the expectation that students will present a module on an upcoming election or on local, national, or regional current events. School-based service learning could be supported by an independent study, a special topics or fieldwork course, or within an existing course as a group assignment.

This form of service learning has several advantages. It is far more predictable and reliable than working with several different community organizations, nonprofit agencies, or offices of local government. It provides students a service experience within a structure with which they are familiar. It can meet a very real need in terms of creating new instructional resources—especially in public schools. It requires students to master a topic in order to teach it to others. It also provides students the opportunity to apply what they are learning, test out their ideas, and to assess and analyze their theories after applying them. Moreover, school-based service learning requires students to collaborate more extensively, thus offering them more opportunity to work in teams.

However, the advantages of this form of service learning can deter students from working for its deeper political significance. The satisfaction of students and teachers may be high enough that there is little incentive to probe into the roles and purposes of public education; the racial makeup of different schools; the race and gender of administrators and teachers; the differences among schools in facilities, equipment, repair and cleanliness, professionalism and dedication of teachers; and the educational future of the students of different schools. But it is precisely in the reflection on these issues about the social provisions for the education of children of different classes and races that we begin to teach democracy.

Action Research

Action research coordinates the information needs of social service organizations with requirements of courses. It provides a specific orientation to internships with community organizations and agencies such as the Catholic Worker, the United Way, or member groups of "the backyard revolution" (Boyte 1980). Such groups can always use talented researchers to assist in fundraising, lobbying, direct action, or advocacy work.

Students can also participate in action research in an independent study project, a term project in a class, or in lengthy student research assignments in capstone or honors courses or thesis seminars. For example, one American Studies student did her senior seminar thesis on landownership in an inner-city neighborhood. In addition to readings on the development of the inner city in the past three decades, she went to city hall and researched owners of every lot in a nine-block square area. She did this work at the request of a community center run by a Catholic parish. The work was needed for the larger goal of neighborhood redevelopment that was part of the vision of the leaders of the community center. So far, her report has been part of neighborhood-wide discussions of two development plans.

This example also illustrates central and distinguishing features of successful action research as service learning. First, it involves independent research by students. Second, that research is requested by a community group or agency and conducted under their supervision. Third, the community agency has a use for the research that it can specify clearly. Fourth, the research is turned over to the community agency for its use.

As noted above, action research may also fit into course requirements for a class. For example, students in a social movement class may work with leaders in a gay and lesbian organization, a domestic violence hotline, an organization of mental health consumers or the physically handicapped, or some similar organization to research an issue or to conduct some other information-gathering action related to its work. Students then satisfy term paper or other research requirements in those classes by addressing the information needs of the agency. For example, the director of the Virginia

Coalition for the Homeless has identified her organization's need to continue the annual census of the homeless in the state and to monitor the hearings of state legislative committees on poverty in Virginia. Students in a state and local government course could couple their classroom work with assignments to monitor, report, and analyze the hearings and recommendations of legislative committees.

Given the size of most action research assignments and the limited time that students have to fulfill one assignment in one class during a single semester, it is useful to organize class members into teams and for team members to break the action research into smaller, discrete parts that can be accomplished in a semester. In this manner, one team in a community leadership course worked with the Richmond AIDS Ministry Program to research care programs during the day for persons with AIDS. Some members of that team traveled to other cities to learn about programs there. Other members researched federal funding sources for such programs. Together, team members prepared a proposal with information on funding sources. Another team in that class worked with an international agency for children to devise effective methods of evaluation, as reports of local projects from national offices around the world varied widely. Students examined them and made suggestions about the current methods of reporting that provide information on the ten goals of children's well-being that the international office had established. They also recommended changes in reporting that would be useful to acquire additional information to track the progress of each project in achieving the ten goals of the agency. Finally, the action research potential afforded our students by access to information on the Internet is boundless.

Action research imparts several democratic lessons. It instructs students in the limits and possibilities of addressing political problems efficaciously. If done in the manner of participatory research, this form of service learning also requires students to listen to one another, to deliberate critically about common problems and issues, to arrive at solutions to mutual problems creatively in a community setting, and perhaps to work together to implement solutions. Obviously, some of these outcomes will be better met than others in the course of a single semester, but their combination is the democratic constellation of which Dewey wrote.

Community Problem Solving (COMPS) Seminar: Putting It All Together

Service learning can also combine classroom work, experiential education, and community service in major new ways. In the Community Problem Solving (COMPS) seminar, students review social problems of the nation, inquire into a particular city's social problems, discuss them and their possible solutions with local leaders, and address one of those problems through service with a community agency or advocacy group. The seminar combines class work, reading, visiting lecturers, field trips, and a twenty to thirty hour weekly internship. This program encourages students to think globally, to act locally, and to combine democratic theory and action. In this way, COMPS extends action research. Students have twenty or more hours a week over a semester to devote to a research issue, permitting them to take on larger issues and to do more work on them (Schott 1994). Some examples of COMPS projects include establishing a computer spreadsheet program for the office of Habitat for Humanity to track mortgage payments of participants; assisting the state Planned Parenthood office develop a program of school-based sex education; and assisting a statewide health agency to establish a program to recognize innovative, community-based health programs.

By themselves, none of these tasks will bring on a new, democratic America but each of them helps construct improved democratic practice—including democratic teaching. When students undertake these tasks they enter an off-campus classroom of popular education on housing policy and class structure; on the influence of race, class, and gender roles on teen pregnancy; and on power within the health care system. They also learn specific, concrete steps to address these problems through individual courage and collective action. These lessons of popular education, in the hands of a skillful teacher-facilitator, complement classroom texts, such as William Julius Wilson's study (1987) of the underclass, to explain social problems, their origins and causes, and specific steps to deal with them. COMPS combines the lessons of democratic critique and improved democratic practice which we spoke about in the Introduction.

Gleanings from student essays at the conclusion of the 1994 COMPS seminar at the University of Richmond suggest its democratic, pedagogical outcomes. Although derived from a very small sample, the responses are representative of other students' comments extending over almost twenty years and more than a thousand students.

Students reported personal development. They became aware of and grappled with: "white guilt" in working with other racial groups; socioeconomic class differences; the benefits and costs of careers they contemplated; different styles of relating to people in various positions of authority and situations (e.g., welcoming new staff members into an organization, volunteering, and meeting commitments). This personal development includes learning skills that extend beyond the classroom. Students reported a better understanding of formal education as related to acquiring skills to be applied in real life rather than for merely passing tests. Others were faced with the social consequences of procrastination, and with their need to exercise more self-direction, initiative, and self-assertion in order to work more effectively with people.

Students reported social and political development. This included lessons about personal trust. How and why is it given? How and why is it acquired? Their reports included lessons they acquired from their work and from observing others with whom they worked about the capacity to affect the lives of people in need. They also learned the cost of time and commitment to exercise this capacity. One student confessed frankly that he was probably not ready to make the commitment that he saw his coworkers and supervisor make. Students acquired a sharper awareness of their differences from other people as individuals and as members of groups, for example, their attitudes toward education or pregnancy as a teenager. On the other hand, they also became more aware of the common bonds they had with people who they took to be different from themselves—such as the formerly homeless man who conducted the walking tour of homelessness for the group through the streets of Richmond one bright and hot May morning. They became aware of the importance and usefulness of networks in bringing about change and left with hope that change is possible.

Perhaps the greatest implications of COMPS for democratic teaching lay in the teacher-facilitators as much as the students. Democratic teaching requires the redistribution of classroom resources, no less than improved democratic practice does in other fields. Service learning, as democratic teaching, redistributes some university resources to people and agencies in the community who would have no benefit from those resources otherwise. If done well, extensive service learning formats, like action research and COMPS, may provide groups with necessary but otherwise unavailable information and with powerful allies for political action. This result may also provide academic institutions a new or more formal role in the community of response. It is altogether possible and fitting that this new role may spark faculty and student deliberation and action about the allocation of resources for its role in the community of response.

The COMPS seminar required a full-time student assistant during the summer semester we conducted it. LINCS now has a staff of two full-time persons, while beginning with one part-time student coordinator. Programs like LINCS and COMPS require resources. Faculty and students have adapted service learning at the University of Richmond because the LINCS staff has assisted them. Acquiring staff for a program like LINCS requires an allocation of new resources or a reallocation of existing ones. In either event, developing resources to improve democratic teaching may, as in this case, require a department, college, or university to rearrange its priorities and redistribute its resources.

Service learning requires the redistribution of power and authority within the classroom as well. The successful integration of service learning into class work requires turning over significant amounts of class time to the students for planning and reporting. Coordinating team members' efforts requires time spent together, and often class members see each other only in class. Likewise, accountability in service learning requires some form of reporting mechanism, such as oral reports, to the class. Use of class time in this fashion turns that time over to the students for their use. It contrasts sharply with traditional methods, especially lecture and class discussion. More generally, service learning requires teachers to redistribute time and attention from themselves, assigned readings, and lectures to the students, their experiences, and the distillation of lessons from discussion.

Delegating control over class time is not an abdication of teaching responsibility but a deliberate pedagogy to foster the community required for problem solving and civic education. The different forms of service learning we have described require varying amounts of class time. A service learning assignment of fifteen hours requires perhaps a class session or limited reference and incorporation in class regularly. COMPS, on the other hand, devotes the largest portion of class time to service learning and reflection upon it. The two forms of service learning have very different ratios of class to service learning time.

COMPS provides students a very intense and extensive service learning experience, with their evaluative comments reflecting that experience. Yet, every form of service learning can provide similar outcomes to some degree. These results, ultimately, are the justification of service learning in the curriculum. They serve the purposes of the curriculum, which are to educate students and to assist in their personal development. To these we have added the component, which many argue has been too-long ignored on American campuses, to prepare students to participate effectively in democratic processes of public problem solving.

SERVICE LEARNING AND CRITICAL THEORY

Service learning, as I conceive it, resembles critical social science in methods and purpose. Both service learning and critical theory imply change and a redistribution of resources. Critical theory assumes that human beings, including students, are agents in history with the capacity to establish more equitable social, economic, and political arrangements. It assumes further that people develop more completely as human beings in environments of freedom. However, that freedom is never complete. The history that people have previously made shapes the current possibilities that they have to create new history. People are acted upon by history as well as being its authors. These assumptions and the efforts to regain the human origins and possibilities within any set of conditions is what Brian Fay (1987) calls critical social science.

Adding critical theory to this analysis suggests that service learning is a means to burrow into the study of politics as well as into the teaching of democracy, with some of this work already done. In particular, action research has deep roots in the social sciences as one method within critical theory. These roots ultimately bloom in varied forms: action science (Argyris, Putnam, and Smith 1985), naturalistic inquiry (Lincoln and Guba 1985), usable knowledge (Lindbloom 1990; Lindbloom and Cohen 1976), and participatory research (Park 1992). These roots are sustained, like the hopes for democratic teaching, by the work of John Dewey that expresses a common epistemology of critical theory and democratic teaching. Action research, in one definition, engages social scientists with participants, students, and community leaders "in a collaborative process of critical inquiry into problems of social practice in a learning context" (Argyris et al. 1985: 236). According to Kurt Lewin, who coined the phrase, action research displays the following characteristics:

- A change experiment on real problems in social systems that focuses on a particular problem and seeks to provide assistance to a client system.
- Iterative cycles of identifying a problem, planning, acting, and evaluating.
- Reeducation to change well established patterns of thinking and acting that express norms and values.
- Challenges to norms and values of the status quo from a perspective of democratic values.
- Contributions to basic knowledge in social science and to social action in everyday life (Argyris et al. 1985:9).

A similar exposition of naturalistic inquiry, usable knowledge, and participatory research would reveal comparable assumptions about knowledge, accountability in research, and a relation of knowledge and power. Such an exposition would confirm the proposition that service learning, expressed in forms like action research, does not take social scientists away from their field of inquiry but puts them in the middle of an interdisciplinary concern with methods of inquiry and their relation to concepts of power and equality that are central to politics. To be consistent then, the goals of civic education that Barber (Barber 1992a; 1992b; Barber and Battistoni 1993), Boyte (1991; 1993), and others (Harkavy 1993) propose involve service learning not only as a means but also as a topic for critical reflection.

The above observation serves both as an encouragement and a caveat for teachers. It encourages educators to adopt service learning as another means to study politics and to relate research and teaching. But it also provides them warning that as a critical theory, service learning will likely threaten some elements of the status quo on campus and in the community. Service learning is not only a means but a topic for critical reflection as well. Teaching democracy inevitably is not only a means but a topic for critical reflection as well. Teaching democracy inevitably invites public discussion of the appropriateness of the status quo and the institutional changes, including service learning, required to make it more democratic.

In this light, service learning does not become an add-on to the curriculum but provides a singularly effective means to achieve the broadest, most essential goals of the college curriculum. These goals include those of the liberal arts, of experiential education, as well as of public service. The task is not to relate service learning to many different aspects of the curriculum but to catalyze unity among disparate goals of the curriculum and to provide a few means to reach several ends simultaneously and efficiently. Service learning provides a means to teach democracy democratically by bringing the community into the classroom in many ways to promote civic education.

REFERENCES

Alpert, Eugene. 1987. "The Internship Journal: Can Academic Quality Be Maintained?" Paper presented at the annual meeting of the American Political Science Association. Chicago, Illinois.

Argyris, Chris, Robert Putnam, and Diana McLain Smith. 1985. *Action Science.* San Francisco: Jossey-Bass Publishers.

Barber, Benjamin R. 1992a. *An Aristocracy of Everyone: The Politics of Education and the Future of America.* New York: Ballantine Books.

———. 1992b. "Going to the Community." *The Civic Arts Review* 5, no. 4 (Fall): 10-12.

——— and Richard Battistoni. 1993. "A Season of Service: Introducing Service Learning into the Liberal Arts Curriculum." *PS: Political Science & Politics* 26, no. 2 (June): 235-40.

Boyte, Harry C. 1980. *The Backyard Revolution.* Philadelphia: Temple University Press.

———. 1991. "Turning on Youth to Politics." *The Nation* (May 13): 626-28.

———. 1993. "What is Citizenship Education?" In *Rethinking Tradition: Integrating Service with Academic Study on College Campuses,* ed. Tamar Y. Kupiec, 63-66. Providence, R.I.: Campus Compact.

Burns, James MacGregor. 1978. *Leadership.* New York: Harper & Row.

Couto, Richard A. 1982. *Streams of Idealism and Health Care Innovation: An Assessment of Service-Learning and Community Mobilization.* New York: Teachers College Press, Columbia University.

———. 1990. "Assessing a Community Setting as a Context for Learning." In *Combining Service and Learning: A Resource Book for Community and Public Service,* vol. 2, ed. Jane C. Kendall, 251-66. Raleigh, N.C.: National Society for Internships and Experiential Education.

———. 1993. "Service Learning in Service to Leadership Studies." In *Rethinking Tradition: Integrating Service with Academic Study on College Campuses,* ed. Tamar Y. Kupiec, 67–71. Providence, R.I.: Campus Compact.

Fay, Brian. 1987. *Critical Social Science: Liberation and Its Limits.* Ithaca, N.Y.: Cornell University Press.

Gamson, Zelda F. and Associates. 1984. *Liberating Education.* San Francisco: Jossey-Bass.

Gaventa, John. 1980. *Power and Powerlessness: Quiescence and Rebellion in an Appalachian Valley.* Urbana: University of Illinois Press.

Harkavy, Ira. 1993. "University-Community Partnerships: The University of Pennsylvania and West Philadelphia as a Case Study." In *Rethinking Tradition: Integrating Service with Academic Study on College Campuses,* ed. Tamar Y. Kupiec, 121-28. Providence, R.I.: Campus Compact.

Honnet, Ellen Porter and Susan J. Poulsen. 1989. "Principles of Good Practice for Combining Service and Learning." *The Wingspread Journal: Special Report.* Racine, Wisc.: The Johnson Foundation, Inc.

Hursh, Barbara. 1990. "Tools for Journals and Debriefing." In *Combining Service and Learning: A Resource Book for Community and Public Service,* vol. 2, ed. Jane C. Kendall, 80-86. Raleigh, N.C.: National Society for Internships and Experiential Education.

Levine, Arthur. 1980. *When Dreams and Heroes Died.* San Francisco: Jossey-Bass.

Lincoln, Yvonne S. and Egon G. Guba. 1985. *Naturalistic Inquiry.* Beverly Hills, Calif.: Sage.

Lindbloom, Charles E. 1990. *Inquiry and Change: The Troubled Attempt to Understand and Shape Society.* New Haven: Yale University Press.

——— and David Cohen. 1976. *Usable Knowledge.* New Haven: Yale University Press.

Park, Peter. 1992. "The Discovery of Participatory Research as a New Scientific Paradigm: Personal and Intellectual Accounts." *The American Sociologist* (Winter): 29-42.

Schott, Cheryl. 1994. *COMPS: Community Problem Solving Seminar Handbook.* Richmond: University of Richmond, LINCS Program.

Stanton, Timothy. 1981. "Discovering the Ecology of Human Organizations: Exercises for Field Study Students." In *Field Study: A Source Book for Experiential Learning,* ed. Lenore Borzak. Beverly Hills, Calif.: Sage Publications.

Wilson, William J. 1987. *The Truly Disadvantaged: The Inner City, the Underclass and Public Policy.* Chicago: University of Chicago Press.

Winter, David C., D. C. McClelland, and A. J. Stewart. 1981. *A New Case for the Liberal Arts: Assessing Institutional Goals and Student Development.* San Francisco: Jossey-Bass.

Zimmerman, Jane, Vicki Zawacki, Jan Bird, Virginia Peterson, and Charles Norman. 1990. "Journals: Diaries for Growth." In *Combining Service and Learning: A Resource Book for Community and Public Service,* vol. 2, ed. Jane C. Kendall, 69-79. Raleigh, N.C.: National Society for Internships and Experiential Education.

4

Applying Democratic Theory in Community Organizations

Richard Guarasci and Craig A. Rimmerman

In this chapter we provide an overview and critique of a team-taught, upper-level political science course entitled "Community, Politics, and Service." The course requires students to be fully engaged in a term-long community service project. Our goals are: (1) to outline the critique of community service, (2) to discuss the goals of the course with particular emphasis on "critical education for citizenship," (3) to explain how we attempted to achieve the course's goals and avoid the pitfalls of community service critics, (4) to discuss where the course fell short in achieving our goals, and (5) to outline the broader implications of our course and the reforms that need to be made in order to avoid these problems in the future.

CITIZEN EDUCATION FOR DISCOURAGED CITIZENS

It is indeed ironic that at the very moment that Eastern Europe is celebrating a transition to a Western-style democracy, we in the United States are becoming increasingly critical of our own. Indeed, two recent books discuss the stalemate of American democracy, *Why Americans Hate Politics* (Dionne 1991) and its betrayal, *Who Will Tell the People* (Greider 1992).

Moreover, the Harwood Group, a public issues research and consulting firm, measured a broad level of citizen disaffection with American politics (Harwood Group 1991). This study, prepared for the Kettering Foundation in 1991, found that Americans do care about politics, but they do not believe that their political participation can have a meaningful effect. Citizens believe that they are politically impotent and are cut off from most policy issues given the way they are framed and represented in public discourse. Finally, the study indicated that citizens believe that many of the avenues open to them for expressing their views are mere window dressing, not serious attempts to hear the public. They believe they can be heard only when they organize into large groups and angrily protest policy decisions.

Those of us in higher education are uniquely situated to evaluate citizen disaffection and to devise strategies rooted in a curriculum that enables our students to grapple with the meaning of citizenship, democracy, and public participation in compelling ways. We have much to offer as we tackle these issues in our teaching, our research, and in our community work. We suggest that a model we call critical, proactive education for democratic citizenship can best achieve our educational goals.

A course rooted in critical, proactive education for democratic citizenship should have the following characteristics:

1. It should present the full critique of American democracy to the student

2. It should allow students to see the importance of participating in public decisions

3. It should ask educators and students to conceive of democracy broadly to include community discussions, community action, public service, and protest politics

4. It should ask students to conceptualize participation very broadly to include workplace and community opportunities for participation

5. It should encourage students to take into account the important relationship among gender, race, and class concerns in the participatory process (i.e., "the politics of difference")

6. It should ask students to confront their assumptions regarding power and leadership as well as the sources of such assumptions (Rimmerman 1993, chapter 6).

THE CRITIQUE OF SERVICE

Many observers believe that public service courses that require students to participate in the community simply cannot achieve all that they advertise by service alone. For example, Harry Boyte writes that "community service is not a cure for young people's political apathy" because "it teaches little about the arts of participation in public life." In addition, it falls far short of providing the everyday connections that students must have to the daily political process. Most courses that require community service also fail to afford students the opportunity that they need "to work effectively toward solving society's problems" (Boyte 1991:766).

Boyte also laments the fact that most student interns avoid tackling larger policy questions and issues. In this sense, they often conceive of service as an alternative to politics. Boyte points out, for example, that the language of community service is infused with the language of "helping" rather than "a vocabulary that draws attention to the public world that extends beyond personal lives and local communities." Service volunteers rarely have the ability to engage the complex intersection of class, race, and power that develop as middle-class youths engage in projects in low-income areas. In the absence of "a conceptual framework that distinguishes between personal life and the public world, community service adopts the 'therapeutic language' that now pervades society" (Boyte 1991:766). It is this therapeutic approach that cannot begin to deal with the inequalities that structure the relationship between the so-called servers and the served. In the end, service activity is devoid of politics and in this sense, it is a relatively empty way of tackling complex structural issues that arise out of the conditions prompting service activity in the first place.

Yet another set of criticisms raises questions of the relationship of the individual to the state. According to Eric Gorham, "Community service is an institutional means by which the state uses political discourse and ideology to reproduce a postindustrial capitalist economy in the name of good citizenship" (Gorham 1992:1). For Gorham and other critics, community service reinforces the worst form of clientelism and tacitly accepts the structural inequalities growing out of the limited American welfare state. It does so by working largely within the confines of our current system without always affording students the opportunity to critique that system in a fundamental way. In this way, it promotes an invidious form of authoritarianism.

Gorham raises other serious, practical considerations that need to be addressed by proponents of any community service, whether educators, citizen volunteers, or student interns. To Gorham, these are the most important questions:

1. How well can the practice of community service fulfill its theoretical goals?
2. What does "inculcating civic education" mean in concrete terms? In what sense will community service offer opportunities for democracy, equality, and participation to those who serve?
3. Is the goal of citizenship appropriate to all people, regardless of their race or gender?
4. Does community service contribute to citizenship in any material way?
5. How should citizenship be nurtured?
6. Do the ideas of the planners of community service coincide with those of the philosophers who might view it as appropriate to their [philosophers'] ends (Gorham 1992:10)?

Critics such as Eric Gorham point out that most proponents of service fail to even ask these questions, and as a result, avoid discussing the kind of theoretical underpinnings that should be at the core of any courses that require students to participate in service activities.

The libertarian perspective offers a final critique of community service programs. Doug Bandow warns, for example, that President Clinton's national service program will ultimately lead to government coercion because all government service programs assume at their core that citizens are not responsible to each other but are responsible to the state. In this way, the "volunteers" are actually coerced by the government to participate in service programs, thus taking away their liberty and freedom (Bandow 1993). Bandow's critique is particularly relevant to the present analysis because it raises interesting questions about whether students should be required to participate in any service experience as part of a college course or courses.

It seems to us that proponents of a curricular-based community service must respond to the above concerns. We do so here within the context of a discussion of our own team-taught course. But before we do so, we provide an overview of the requirements of our course and the connection between course readings and the community service requirement.

COURSE OVERVIEW

Partially in response to issues raised by the critics of service learning, we designed a course that explicitly placed citizenship at its center. In fact, the initial problem for this course is: "In a multicultural democracy what does citizenship come to mean and what educational preparation is required for its development and enhancement?"

To engage this question critically, we thought it imperative to account for the sociological and cultural experiences of undergraduates both on our campus and in the nation. Their arrival from "the real world" (as some characterize life outside the academy) carries with it all the provincialism, ethnocentrism, and cultural myths circumscribed within their civic and personal biographies.

According to Andrew Hacker, virtually 80 percent of African-American high school students in New York City attend de facto segregated high schools, and an almost equal number of white suburbanites in the New York City metropolitan area attend equally segregated schools (Hacker 1992). When many of these students attend college they arrive on campus as virtual strangers to one another. For the most part they are prisoners of their particular socioethnic pasts and they are likely to encounter meaningful and sustained racial and ethnic diversity for the first time in their lives.

In this context, social differences are, at best, tolerated. Normally, students are only capable of constructing a social world composed of a crude version of new and unfamiliar cultural relations. This leads to a secure but somewhat isolated set of racial and ethnic enclaves on campus, not unlike the very worlds from which the students have migrated. Consequent to this social arrangement, political and social marginalization is sustained within the campus community, and it should be of little surprise when this type of cultural milieu produces harmful and wounding racial and ethnic conflicts.

Situated within this social context, it became evident to us that real democratic citizenship, first and foremost, is learned and not inherited. It is not to be found within the ethos of students' personal experiences or their limited exposure within public and community institutions. And even more critically, intercultural experience is almost absent in the face of a society now reaffirming and relegitimizing the impenetrability of racial, ethnic, and other social differences. The primary function of our course (and hopefully a sequence of courses) would be to connect issues of democratic participation, social difference, and critical judgment with an emerging need for a vibrant sense of intercultural citizenship. Our work was to help students understand their interdependence and to begin to develop the critical capacities for imagining the possibilities of an intercultural and multicentric democracy, where community and difference would become synergistic and generative, not isolating and degenerative (as it is at present).

Thus, the efficacy of public and community service rests with the fusion of formal learning and community involvement. For students, public and community service holds the possibility of dissolving the old and false dualities between campus life and "the real world." Through sustained personal involvement with community institutions and persons in need, service learning helps our students demystify "the other," those outside of their immediate social experience. It assists them in creating a reservoir of personal experience that makes real and compelling the everyday lives faced by individuals, institutions, and communities subordinated by political and economic fences that shut off resources that would address their needs. In short, service learning and community involvement hold out the possibility for making real the personal and the political by establishing an ethical harbinger for what Paulo Freire calls "a pedagogy of hope" (Freire 1970).

Service learning likely will not play this role if it ultimately disconnects issues of social justice from those of social transformation and political empowerment. As Robert Coles cogently warns, community service is always vulnerable to the exercise of *noblesse oblige,* social voyeurism, and elitism (Coles 1993). This is particularly true when service is totally estranged from moral, ethical, and ultimately intellectual dialogues that allow critical reflection and group dialogue to emerge within the community and among groups of community volunteers. Isolated and individualized acts of altruism are not unimportant in the scheme of things, but as singular and privatized acts they remain outside of a public dialogue about the existential, ethical, and political realities of the community and the curriculum. As such, disconnected service is more likely than immersed community service to unwittingly leave students with a greater sense of the intractability of social and personal problems and, at best, reproduce a sense of elitist obligation.

To combat these undesirable outcomes, service learning must help students connect ideas and experience. Service learning must be about helping students enlarge their understanding of their community experience by enveloping it in rich and diverse readings that carefully link democratic critique with democratic possibility. In this way, community service becomes part of a powerful learning frame for students and reaches well beyond the immediate service course. This is better accomplished with community service that provides students with experience that relates critically and supportively to the readings and the course dialogues. Course-embedded community service begins to introduce students to the practice of joining ideas and values, or what some traditional educators may term "liberal learning" and others more closely associated with progressive and popular educational movements would label "the development of a political imagination."

In an age of a vigorous and regenerative social segmentation, community service and service learning of this type can become the critical underpinnings of an ethical foundation necessary for any new progressive democratic politics. Without a moral domain, citizenship can be reduced to a selfish act of possessive individualism. Without developing what Alexis de Tocqueville, and later Robert Bellah et al. (1985), have so aptly termed "the habits of the heart," renewed calls for political education exclusively focused on learning the "acts of democracy" are more likely to reproduce the politics of the present. This is a political atmosphere in which self-interest replaces a democratic and civic sensibility, and single issue and interest group politics becomes a substitute for the hard work of coalition building and the nurturing of "common ground." Without an experience *in* the community, it is unlikely that a renewed political education movement would be *with* and *for* the community.

GENEVA, N.Y.: A MICROCOSM OF POSTINDUSTRIAL AMERICA

Our course is entitled "Politics, Community, and Service" and has no prerequisites, although approximately half of the thirty students enrolled are political science majors at Hobart and William Smith Colleges. The substance of the course is its focus on the antinomies of American democracy and racial and social difference, and also the problem of envisioning and constructing a viable, intercultural democratic community. The role of the citizen within this larger participatory and inclusive politics is much broader than either the classical or contemporary colloquial understandings of citizenship. The course asks students to interrogate critically and to reconstruct the meanings of difference, community, and democracy in a time when they seem hopelessly unrelated and irreconcilable.

To understand the educational efficacy of the service learning component of the course, one must understand the political economy of Geneva, New York, where Hobart and William Smith Colleges is located. The city serves as a genuine metaphor for many of the racial, ethnic, and class differences found throughout the nation.

Geneva, New York, is first a rural city, itself enigmatic. It sustains at least several different epochs of American economic history. A sizeable portion of its socioeconomic composition is agrarian. In addition to traditional farming, much of the surrounding area is dotted with a number of vineyards and wineries that employ an extensive migrant work force, mostly Latino. The city proper benefitted until the last decade from a vibrant industrial base of manufacturing firms. The service sector is mostly framed around wholesale and retail franchises that provide low-paying, unsecured employment with very few, if any, benefits. Finally, a growing underground street economy is emerging, founded on illegal drug activities and supported by a seemingly nomadic population.

Socially, Geneva is populated by a diversity of ethnic and racial groups. Since the antebellum period, African Americans have settled in Geneva. Originally brought to the area by rich Virginians spending their summers on the shores of Seneca Lake, they ultimately benefitted from the emergence of a section in the underground railroad in Geneva, and have long maintained a significant presence in the area. With the advent of mass production industries after the Civil War, European immigrants, mostly of Italian ancestry, came to Geneva in large numbers. They now constitute the largest portion of the population and dominate the political structure of the city. In addition, Asian, Latin, and other European groups are represented in significant numbers in Geneva's population.

An extreme class-segmented society, racially diverse and characterized by rural agricultural, migrant, manufacturing service, and underground workers, Geneva captures a sense of diversity remarkable for upstate New York, particularly for a small community. It is a city suffering miserably from deindustrialization and it has not found a path to economic prosperity in the "globally competitive" economy. The content of our course—democracy, diversity, and the composition of a hypersegmented community in economic eclipse—provided a natural coordinate point for the larger project of citizenship education.

THE PEDAGOGY OF THE COURSE

The course is about democracy, community, and difference. It requires that students be fully engaged in a term-long community service project. The course asks students to be fully engaged in the biographies of people within the community and to be involved in writing autobiographically about the effect of their service on their own lives, their perspective on democracy, and their understanding of democratic citizenship.

The course prizes independent thought, focusing on the critical evaluation of both the readings and the field experience and how each serves to illuminate the other. Students are asked to reaffirm one central precept, namely, that learning requires a serious commitment to both the subject at hand, and the voices and experiences of those engaged in the course and the community.

Students are involved in community service from two perspectives. First, Geneva is a community in need of serious assistance as it encounters the limits, contradictions, and dramatic changes surrounding the realities of postmodern capitalism. Service learning involves students in the everyday lives of persons who are often cornered by a very limited menu of social and economic choices. The experiences of Geneva residents and the students' experiences with them, are authentic and real unto themselves. We work with residents to enhance positive change in their immediate circumstances, the work of empowerment and social transformation.

Some of our students were fortunate to experience this positive change directly. Several students revitalized the efforts of the local literacy program, working with individuals and families. Some of this work involved collaboration with migrant workers in the local wineries and vineyards. Literacy work was completed in both Spanish and English. By addressing both adults and children, literacy efforts had profound impacts on personal self-esteem, individual competency, and collective initiative in addressing the needs of a socially, politically, and economically marginalized migrant population.

Second, service learning is, itself, a project in citizenship. At the very least, it is a citizenship project if it explores the nature and limits of democratic citizenship in our time. This component of service learning is an essential and quite important commitment in its own right. What does citizenship mean in today's America? What should it mean? How does it relate to various perspectives on justice? Democracy? Community? Difference? Service learning ideally allows us to rethink these basic and critical concepts.

From both perspectives in service learning—social change and democratic citizenship—students need to bring together the experiential with the intellectual (Barber and Battistoni 1993). Both experience and ideas are ways to know the world, and our goal is to create a pedagogy—a way to learn— that joins the course readings with field experience so that students can use each of these aspects to understand and critically evaluate the other. Toward this goal, we are attempting to end the narrow approach to education that separates learning from experience. That perspective limits learning simply to the acquisition and absorption of knowledge. We are also attempting to end the equally false dualism of separating knowledge from personal experience. The goal of this course is to reconcile these different realms of learning by joining readings and experience, intellectual development and ethical growth, and our individual academic experience with the unfolding of our own larger autobiographies.

WRITING, READING, AND DOING: THE JOURNAL, THE ETHNOGRAPHY, AND THE AUTOBIOGRAPHY

Communication, experience, and reflection are the means to intellectual and ethical growth. In this course, we are constantly engaged in all three in ways that bring faculty and students together so that we can share, compare, and contrast our thoughts and feelings. To these ends, the course assignments are meant to provide mechanisms for communication and reflection allowing us to both *personally* engage the content (readings and service) and to begin creating a community of learning *within* the course. The assignments both in and outside of class are meant to help us collaborate so that we can expand our personal understanding of our experience and to begin to see our involvement as a collective and cooperative enterprise in which we genuinely learn from one another.

Each student must regularly use a journal for this class, but a very special type of journal. We are looking for personal, idiosyncratic notation, and we want students to write insightful and reflective reviews (not reports) of what they find to be key aspects of the assigned readings. In addition, we want them to write about their field experience in some detail, but also in contrast and comparison to the readings. What do they have in common or in opposition, or both? Finally, we want them to read one anothers' journals so that they can share their ideas and experiences. We will call our type of journal a dialogical experiential journal.

In addition, students are asked to write two analytic, argumentative papers in which they critically evaluate many of the course readings and the central arguments of the assigned authors. Two additional assignments, along with several required submissions of the journal for review, make the writing assignments more integrative of the course readings with the field experience. One is a required ethnographic portrait of a community person encountered in the field work. Here students are asked to be intelligent observers as well as participants in the community. They meet persons whose lives tell a story about one or more key aspects of community life: class, ethnicity, race, gender, power and powerlessness, empowerment and subordination, and other forms of social difference. They encounter the circumstances of material shortcomings, the anxieties brought on by semipermanent economic vulnerability, and stories of great courage in overcoming seemingly insurmountable obstacles. In this assignment, we ask students to grasp that they too are authors with important insights regarding the telling of the personal story of another significant person. The assigned works from Robert Coles (1993), Studs Terkel (1992), Gloria Anzaldua (1987), and Audre Lorde (1984), provide excellent sources for this work.

The final writing assignment is an intellectual and ethical citizen autobiography. We ask the students to reflect explicitly upon their experience with the authors, the course discussions, and their community involvement as one "text" to be engaged, assessed, and evaluated. "How has the class helped you reexamine your personal, ethical, and political values?" "What does service learning do for your understanding of democratic citizenship?" In short, we ask them to tell us (and themselves) who they are by virtue of what they believe, what they do, and what they have read. By joining action to knowledge and reflection, we ask our students to consciously become the subjects of democracy, political actors in and around a community in which they are intimately involved. In its most brilliant moments, service learning develops in our students the democratic imagination and personal commitments required of active citizens.

One poignant example involved a student working with a local food group distributing needed groceries to low-income individuals and families. She wrote extensively in her journal and her citizen autobiography about her intense feelings of guilt and her privileged position in society in contradiction to the plight of the people she worked alongside. She came from a middle-income family in New England, a family of liberal viewpoints and keen sensitivity to the needs of others, yet she experienced deep anxiety about her own feelings of social distance and privilege. Ultimately, she came to the realization that society placed "borders," as she put it, around all social differences and these borders were largely irrelevant on a personal basis. She wrote about her realization of how the "self-other" dichotomy is socially created.

I had trouble overcoming the stereotypes and fears dictated by society about poor people. I had, without realizing it, internalized these stereotypes so that they affected my perceptions of these people.

I realize now that the anxiety and guilt I felt on that first day at the Food Pantry was a result of the fact that, deep down, I was being forced to recognize and confront my fear that I would be blamed for the living conditions of these people who I did not even know. When, to my surprise, I was accepted without judgment by the majority of the people I met at the Food Pantry, I was able to let go of my guilt and fear enough to accept and engage our differences, thus bridging the gap between us.

This is the very same process that Audre Lorde describes in her book, *Sister Outsider*. With that insight, now she is capable of sustaining a full commitment to social activism and personal involvement regardless of the uneasiness of the social setting. She has learned that the disquieting aspect of traversing class difference is an artificial barrier to human connection. In her own words, "Boundaries serve no purpose other than to keep people separated so that they do not have to see how their everyday actions and decisions necessarily impact on others." This was a remarkable existential breakthrough, aided by the conjunction of the readings, the field work, and the writing.

FIELD WORK

We have had students engaged as volunteers in a wide variety of community projects, from literacy programs and the local food pantry to active work with the rape crisis center and the neighborhood watch associations. On average, they worked between three to five hours per week over a ten-week term. Our office of community service programs helped with placements, field assessment, and overall logistical support.

Individual student experience varied among the sites. Some students had major encounters with their own value systems, while others had rather routine involvement with the agencies. One young woman working with a women's organization confronted issues of sexual abuse that resonated with her own personal experience. Her dialogical journal represented deep reflection about the readings, particularly those discussing issues of gender and difference as well as those analyzing conditions of empowerment. While her field experience was deeply personal, it was not so qualitatively different from that of many of the students. Most everything related to reflective discussions about issues of equity, justice, and care. For almost all of the students, this was their first opportunity to frame their community work in a larger context of rigorous intellectual work and group reflection.

Other students encountered firsthand some of the fundamental social barriers to ethnic and racial harmony within the community. Working with neighborhood improvement groups, they witnessed the deeply encoded racial antagonism that surrounds issues such as the inclusion of low-income tenants, usually Latino or African American, in neighborhood efforts to increase safety and to start cleanup campaigns. To some of the more economically secure residents, welfare recipients and low-income groups *were* the problem they wanted to solve. They viewed single-parent, poor families as spawning grounds for crime and neighborhood decay. Our students came to these tensions as more naive initiates, and at first were bewildered as to how to deal with the obvious biases. After a time, they would gently but forthrightly state their desire to help everyone in the neighborhood and to create bridges where possible. As one student said,

Regardless of the can of worms I'm about to open, one cannot truly understand something without experiencing it. [Local resident] may be disgusted with the housing of the poor, but he could never understand their situations until he walked in their shoes for a day. Service within your community opens the lines of communication because you begin to experience that which you have never had the opportunity to experience before, whether it is positive or negative.

Thus, the depth of racial and class divisions became very real to them and, for most, increased their determination to engage them as effectively as possible. This is in stark contrast to many of their uninvolved college associates who remain largely unaware or nihilistic about the omniscient nature of such social conflicts, and accordingly see politics as something remote to their personal lives. As another student wrote,

Perhaps one of the most important revelations I've had about democratic citizenship as a result of this class is that it is based upon the conviction that there are extraordinary possibilities in ordinary people (Harry Emerson Fosdick).

Through all of the readings and my service, I discovered the extraordinary possibilities within myself. This discovery led to my departure from civic and communal disconnection and dedication to civic and communal connection . . .

Although this redefinition of self was frightening and frustrating, as it seemed to rob me of stability and certainty, I, like Lorde, began to recognize a source of power within myself that comes from the knowledge that while it is most desirable not to be afraid, learning to put fear into a perspective gave me great strength. (Lorde 41).

. . . I will use this strength to bring forth and act on the extraordinary possibilities within me throughout the remainder of my life

CRITICAL REFLECTIONS ON THE COURSE

Throughout our course, some students were reluctant to relate the course reading and discussion materials to politics and broader issues of democracy and citizenship. There are several possible explanations for their unwillingness to do so. First, it is possible that we, as faculty facilitators, were not tough enough in forcing our students to make the appropriate connections. Yet this is difficult to do in a course that is rooted in participatory democratic principles. Second, there can be little doubt that most of our students have been socialized to accept the basic elements of American democracy. However, a critical education for citizenship requires students to reflect on and question these basic elements. We should not be surprised that some students resist engaging in this important critical process. Third, as Harry Boyte and others have pointed out, it may well be that there is a flaw in the structure and nature of courses requiring service to the extent that they fail to connect it appropriately to issues of democracy, politics, and citizenship. Some of our students probably resisted discussing these issues because, in their minds, their service activities had little relevance or connection to them. In addition, some of our students may hold antidemocratic or elitist attitudes, views that make them fundamentally hostile to the participatory democratic vision.

We are also convinced that one course cannot possibly tackle issues of democracy, citizenship, diversity, and difference with the level of depth and attention to detail that such important concerns deserve. As discussed earlier, a central question underlying our course is: How are democracy, citizenship, diversity, difference, and multiculturalism connected to and/or disconnected from one another? One cannot just assume that these connections will be readily apparent to all students. Participation in service learning affords students an opportunity to confront some of these concerns, but it is in the classroom that the difficult task of making important connections must take place. One ten-week course cannot possibly do justice to the magnitude of the issues raised by service learning and the literature on democracy, citizenship, and service.

Our course would surely have been strengthened had it included a greater opportunity for formal community assessment. The service literature is replete with suggestions that members of the community be brought into the course planning, implementation, and evaluation processes. We were not able to do so as much as we had liked, largely because this was the first time such a course was taught and we wanted to get students out into the community as quickly as possible. Students did undergo training, but did not have an opportunity to get feedback from community members prior to and after entering the field. This is a problem that we intend to address over time as the community, the faculty, and our students become more comfortable with service learning, and as more resources become available for the kind of developed campus-wide service learning program that we hope to institute at Hobart and William Smith Colleges.

Finally, one of the justifiable concerns with service-based courses is that students' community experiences end once the formal class is over. It might appear, then, to all involved that students only participate in service learning to fulfill a course requirement. Ideally, all students who participate in service learning courses will continue with their community participation long after the formal course concludes. This was certainly the case for about one-third of our students. Indeed, these students found the service experience so personally rewarding, enriching, and supportive of their work in the classroom that they wanted to make it an important part of their educational experience long after the course was over. But others did terminate their service participation as soon as our course ended. In order to deal with this problem, we need to develop an appropriate institutional structure outside of formal courses that will encourage students to continue with their community service participation. We are currently attempting to develop such a structure on our campus.

CONCLUSION

In his recent book, Benjamin Barber concludes that "the successful resuscitation of the idea of service will not proceed far without the refurbishing of the theory and practice of democratic citizenship, which must in turn become any successful service program's guiding spirit" (Barber 1992:236). In embracing Barber's notion, this chapter has attempted to link critical education for citizenship with community service. Our course provides empirical evidence that active notions of democracy, the public, and citizenship can at times be enhanced though requiring students to engage in community service. Our hope is that the course we have described in this chapter makes the important and required link between theories of democracy and citizenship and community service. Indeed, we should celebrate the strengths of various approaches to citizenship education and allow them to inform us as we develop a critical, proactive pedagogy, a pedagogy that will challenge the prevailing passivity and cynicism of our time.

Indeed, if we do not move to change our pedagogy in universities to compensate for the glaring inadequacies and pressing dangers in the seriously undemocratic structure and process in the "real America" we may be losing the last, best chance our society has to save itself. For if the future leaders of America do not have an appreciation of multicultural diversity in the United States, who will? And if they don't learn appreciation for our democratic process in our colleges—by practice, experience, and serious reflection—where and how will they learn it?

REFERENCES

Anzaldua, Gloria. 1987. *Borderlands: The New Mestiza-La Frontera*. New York: Aunt Lute Books.

Bandow, Doug. 1993. "National Service: Utopias Revisited." *Policy Analysis*. The Cato Institute 190 (March 15): 1-15.

Barber, Benjamin. 1992. *An Aristocracy of Everyone: The Politics of Education and the Future of America*. New York: Ballantine.

Barber, Benjamin and Richard Battistoni. 1993. "A Season of Service: Introducing Service Learning into the Liberal Arts Curriculum." *PS: Political Science & Politics* 26, no. 2 (June): 235-40.

Bellah, Robert N., Richard Madsen, William M. Sullivan, Ann Swindler, and Steven M. Tipton. 1985. *Habits of the Heart: Individualism and Commitment in American Life*. Berkeley: University of California Press.

Boyte, Harry C. 1991. "Community Service and Civic Education." *Phi Delta Kappan* (June): 765-67.

Coles, Robert. 1993. *The Call to Service: A Witness to Idealism*. Boston: Houghton Mifflin.

Dionne, E. J., Jr. 1991. *Why Americans Hate Politics*. New York: Simon and Schuster.

Friere, Paulo. 1970. *Pedagogy of the Oppressed*. New York: Continuum Publishing Co.

Gorham, Eric B. 1992. *National Service Citizenship and Political Education*. Albany: State University of New York Press.

Greider, William. 1992. *Who Will Tell the People: The Betrayal of American Democracy*. New York: Simon and Schuster.

Hacker, Andrew. 1992. *Two Nations: Black and White, Separate, Hostile, Unequal*. New York: Scribner's.

Harwood Group, The. 1991. *Citizens and Politics: A View from Main Street America*. Dayton, Ohio: The Kettering Foundation.

Lorde, Audre. 1984. *Sister Outsider*. Freedom, Calif.: The Crossing Press Feminist Series.

Rimmerman, Craig A. 1993. *Presidency by Plebiscite: The Reagan-Bush Era in Institutional Perspective*. Boulder, Colo.: Westview Press.

Terkel, Studs. 1992. *Race*. New York: New Press.

PART III

Innovative Democratic Institutions within the University

Any form of democratic teaching and practice comes with a parcel of problems for the teacher, the students, and the outside community, too. As the adage goes, "No good deed goes unpunished." We might add, doing democracy is not for the fainthearted or softheaded. It takes a lot of grit and determination plus a big pinch of luck to be able to count the experiment as a complete success.

However, there is an extra measure of trouble for teachers who try to build from scratch a university-based organization that is explicitly democratic in values and practice and designed to involve and serve the outside community. How can such a program "pay" the students for their work? How can it be done in one course? What means are available to market the program in the outside community? Why would outside professionals trust a student-run organization to help them solve "real life" problems? Where will the money come from to pay for telephones, stationery, office space, and all the prerequisites for a successful governmental, nonprofit, or commercial enterprise? Are undergraduate, or even graduate, students up to such a challenge? Are academics, notorious for being impractical dreamers, up to handling hard realities like budgets and personnel problems?

We know of two successful experiments along these lines. Both were attempted at the University of Hawaii's main campus in Honolulu in the late 1970s and early 1980s. Both were the brainchildren of Ted Becker and Christa Daryl Slaton who cofounded and coordinated each project.

Their experience answers all of the above questions, "Yes." There were ways to accomplish all of the objectives within a reasonable period of time. Students learned a lot about democratic theory and the travails of putting it into practice. The community—the state of Hawaii, the city and county of Honolulu, and numerous public and private agencies—sought and received a high-quality service for free.

The University of Hawaii was also a beneficiary, as all public universities have community outreach and public service as a major part of their educational mission. Here, for a nominal cost, the university had a highly visible, innovative "extension" service that did something that no other institution or business—public or private—was doing.

However, to be perfectly candid, those who gained the most from the entire process were the two teachers, Becker and Slaton. As their chapters reveal, they learned the most and felt the greatest sense of accomplishment. Moreover, through the two organizations, which their chapters describe and which were directed and staffed chiefly by undergraduate students, Becker and Slaton came to appreciate the value of serendipity in experiential action research. Finally, they highly recommend their models to anyone who wants to help democratize the future of America and/or help resolve the seemingly endless spiral of violence in the United States while, at the same time, closely interacting in a personally and professionally rewarding way with their students.

5

The Community Mediation Service: A Model for Teaching Democracy and Conflict Resolution

Christa Daryl Slaton

During the mid-1970s extensive experimentation began on ways to reform the legal system and to examine nonadversarial methods of resolving conflicts. The impetus for change came from multiple factors, which included clogged courts, expensive and lengthy litigation, distrust of lawyers, dissatisfaction of both winners and losers with outcomes, and increase in the types and number of interpersonal conflicts submitted to courts for resolution. The Community Mediation Service, established within the University of Hawaii at Manoa, was created in this era of dissatisfaction and innovation, in 1979, and operated as a research laboratory to study the capacity of students and residents of the surrounding community to learn conflict resolution skills and democratic methods of mediation.

FIND AN ALTERNATIVE TO THE COURTS

Criticisms of the inability of courts to handle the demands placed upon them came from judges, lawyers, professional organizations, litigants, and those who were unable to have their conflicts resolved there. Recommendations for reform ranged from major institutional change to expansion of the status quo by increasing the number of courts and judges. One area of consensus emerged out of the malaise—the view that adversarial methods of resolving conflict are often ineffective or even deleterious to solving interpersonal disputes between persons with an ongoing relationship.

Griffin Bell, attorney general in the Carter administration, advocated the establishment of alternative dispute resolution centers across the country.

These centers, referred to as neighborhood justice centers (NJCs), often relied on lay volunteers in the community who served as mediators in conflicts between residents. Not only was there a reform emphasis on experimenting with nonadversarial means, but also on decentralizing some conflict resolution back into local communities. This also involved deprofessionalizing those empowered to resolve conflicts among citizens.

In the late 1970s, the U.S. Justice Department funded three pilot projects to demonstrate the capacity of three different models of NJCs to resolve conflicts economically, efficiently, and satisfactorily.[1] At the same time, private foundations began to experiment with programs that offered even greater democratization of the adjudication process and decentralization of conflict resolution.

A University of Hawaii faculty member and graduate student conducted comprehensive research prior to seeking funds for the university-based NJC. They searched and analyzed the available literature and research reports on existing centers in the United States. They made field trips to three sites and interviewed directors, staff, and mediators to evaluate the various models and to determine which model might function best in a multicultural environment with exclusive student and volunteer staffing. The investigation of NJCs revealed three major approaches emerging in the alternative dispute resolution movement and significant disagreements among the practitioners of the different models regarding merits and drawbacks. After an evaluation of the three major models, the university researchers designed a fourth model—the university-based Community Mediation Service (CMS)—which is staffed by faculty and students who mediate in cooperation with community volunteers. The uniqueness of the university-based model becomes clear when compared with previously existing models that influenced the design of the Community Mediation Service.

NEIGHBORHOOD JUSTICE CENTER MODELS

Proponents of neighborhood justice centers hold disparate views on the functions and purposes of the new conflict resolution centers. For example, if the emphasis is on how mediation can lessen the caseload of local court systems, then the professionals in the legal systems and/or judicial administration retain control of the center and the processes. Holding this view, they would likely prefer that the mediation service operate out of the courthouse, the prosecutor's office, or some other court-affiliated institution.

Other proponents emphasize the transfer of mediation skills to local community members as a means of decentralizing official power. In other words, there are those who see community-oriented mediation as a mode of reversing and/or reducing the general social trends leading to the massive psychological alienation and powerlessness that result in increased frustration and violence.

These widely disparate aims result in decidedly differing concepts of referral sources, mediation processes, modus operandi for office processes, staffing, location of center, and so forth, among proponents and organizers of NJCs. The three models described below demonstrate the contrasts and similarities of the early prototypes.

Agency Model

Agency-model NJCs usually function as adjuncts to established legal departments or organizations of the local or state government. These centers have been sponsored by courts (the Miami Citizen Dispute Settlement Program), a city manager's office (the Kansas City Neighborhood Justice Center), and county government (the Santa Clara Neighborhood Mediation and Conciliation Service).

Often the primary goal of these centers is to reduce the workload and costs of the organization sponsoring the project. Emphasis is placed on decreased expense for the courts and police and efficiency in handling disputes. Tax dollars pay for staff, administrative costs, and facilities. Government officials, therefore, must justify the use of funds for the NJC rather than other services demanded by the citizens. This justification comes in terms of cost effectiveness and the bulk processing of cases.

Community Model

Community-model centers have been funded by private organizations or individuals. They rely primarily upon control of operations and cases coming directly into the center from the community. The San Francisco Community Board Program, sponsored by nonprofit organizations, is the best known of the early centers. There are other lesser-known and less well-funded operations of the "homespun" mediation variety.[2]

Emphasis in these centers is placed on the value of decentralization of power, return of control regarding major decisions to the community, and increasing cooperation and community awareness among the local residents. Caseloads are considerably lower under these models because the primary goal is to pass on new skills to private citizens and/or help organize communities to solve their own problems. Costs vary considerably depending on the degree of dependency on volunteers and the goals of the center, which may stress community building, as well as conflict resolution.

Agency-Affiliated Community Model

Agency-affiliated community models function under a philosophy that gained widespread popularity during the Reagan and Bush administrations. In this view, private organizations can handle matters more effectively and efficiently than government institutions or agencies. Government agencies provide funding or cases or other means of support to the private organization hoping that it will decrease the workload of the government agency and that the organization will handle the workload in a more efficient manner.

Centers operating under this model include the Rochester Community Dispute Services Project, operated by the American Arbitration Association; the Institute for Mediation and Conflict Resolution Dispute Center in New York City; and the Atlanta Neighborhood Justice Center, operated by a private nonprofit group specifically incorporated to sponsor the program. Private organizations run these centers, but they rely primarily on the support of government agencies for money and referrals. As in the agency model, this model emphasizes cost efficiency and reduction of court caseload.

There are varying ways of relating to the community in programs of this model. For example, the Los Angeles pilot project in Venice/Del Mar put a much greater emphasis on public relations and advertising within its area of operation than did other federally funded projects. Thus, its caseload was not as heavy, but it had a much higher percentage of people walking into its offices from the street than did other federally funded centers in Atlanta and Kansas City that relied on court referrals.

THE NEIGHBORHOOD JUSTICE CENTER PROJECT OF THE UNIVERSITY OF HAWAII

The Community Mediation Service (CMS) at the University of Hawaii was a hybrid of the agency-affiliated community model role. It established a mutually beneficial relationship between the university as an agency and the community. CMS was also unique because it incorporated the university curriculum into its operations—coursework that taught democracy by being democratic.

Undergraduate Classroom Simulations: Litigation vs. Mediation

A precursor to the CMS at the University of Hawaii was a two-year research project on mediation centers in the United States—the Neighborhood Justice Center Project. Initially, the political science researchers sought to identify the criticisms of the American legal system and to examine the impetus behind the creation of mediation centers. To contrast the differences in approaches, they conducted simulation projects in undergraduate classes to demonstrate adversarial methods in court proceedings and nonadversarial practices in mediation. Students were asked to compare the techniques, outcomes, and feelings of participants in litigation and mediation.

Students were amazed at the animosity, antagonism, and anger that were aroused in their simulations of the "winner-take-all" procedures of the courtroom. The opposing "lawyers" developed a spontaneous hostility toward one another during the process. Using the same facts, the role-playing participants were then put into the mediation mode. They began as very hostile—yelling, accusing, and striving to win. As the mediation simulation continued, the disputants began to calm down, even admitting some errors and taking responsibility for some of the problem. The outcome was a compromise reached by the disputants, to the amazement of the entire class. The faculty extended the research project to include graduate students the following semester.

Graduate Seminar in "Courts and Politics"

The graduate students in the seminar Courts and Politics, established a research agenda to determine whether there was a favorable attitudinal climate for a neighborhood justice center in Hawaii and to get some expert and community input into developing the design of a center useful to Hawaii's multicultural society.

The class developed informational packets and mailed them to thirty-two neighborhood boards (county planning advisory boards composed of elected citizens). A number of the boards invited the students to attend public meetings to make presentations about NJCs and to listen to the concerns and ideas of the community residents.

Students presented materials on NJCs in the United States and other countries. At the conclusion of their discussions with the community residents, they handed out surveys to determine: the level of support for an NJC; the types of cases citizens wanted handled in an NJC; and the types of government agencies, if any, the respondents wanted involved in the NJC. The survey results demonstrated broad-based citizen support for neighborhood justice centers. The next step in the NJC project was a conference of government officials and citizen activists at the university's East-West Center in February 1979.

University-Sponsored Conference for Government Officials and Community Activists

The East-West Center meeting on NJCs was small and informal. Attending were some observers from the Honolulu Police Department, Office of the Prosecutor, some representatives from a few of the neighborhood boards, faculty, and students. The conference led to a series of joint planning meetings between the university NJC Project and a newly formed NJC subcommittee of a neighborhood board in very close geographical proximity to the University of Hawaii.

The meetings that followed the conference centered on discussions among community residents, students, and faculty on the kind of center that should be established; the types of disputes it would handle; how to select mediators; and how to fund and staff it.

The university agreed to sponsor a major conference on campus to bring together representatives of successful U.S. NJCs, noted mediation researchers, and key justice system officials. Faculty donated funds to pay for professional mediation training of students, faculty, and community volunteers.

In the four months of planning for the conference and the establishment of the NJC in Hawaii, a fundamental disagreement developed between a group led by the faculty and a community lawyer who had chaired the planning sessions. The lawyer wanted an appointed board of directors for the NJC to determine the policies of the center. The board would be selected from government and business elites in the community, which he felt would impress potential funders (foundations or government). He also preferred a well-paid professional staff and volunteer mediators with professional backgrounds.

The university researchers, students, and the vast majority of community residents argued for a democratically run center, with a board of directors composed of volunteer staff and mediators. They also contended that the mediators needed to reflect the cultural diversity of Hawaii and should not be restricted to a professional class. The lawyer was unyielding and rejected continued university involvement in planning his elite model. The university group, with substantial support from community residents and two years of advance planning, at that point decided to experiment with an entirely different model than any that had existed previously. The University of Hawaii Law School and the College of Arts and Sciences provided funds for a full-scale educational conference on the various NJCs in the United States. Attended by lawyers, judges, police, legislators, students, and concerned citizens, the conference featured Dan McGillis, a Harvard professor who has written extensively on U.S. mediation centers; Paul Rupert, deputy director of the San Francisco Community Board Program; and Jeff Jefferson, vice president in charge of training at the Institute of Mediation and Conflict Resolution, New York City. The purpose of the conference was to stimulate interest in the NJC being created at the university and to open discussion and debate about other models, with their widely differing goals and procedures.

Immediately following the statewide conference, Jefferson offered a forty-hour, panel-method mediation training to fourteen volunteers. This group became the nucleus of the first NJC in Hawaii—the CMS. Half of the first group of trained mediators came from the university and half came from the outside community (a lawyer, a policeman, a housewife, a retired government employee, an unemployed Hawaiian activist, and two social workers). Of the 50 percent of university mediators, half were undergraduate students.

The democratic coalition of community volunteers, students, and faculty behind CMS decided to offer their services islandwide. Its goal as a one-year model project was to serve as a training ground for those who chose to move out into different areas of the state to establish centers fitting the specific needs of their neighborhoods.

The lawyer led a smaller group to establish a center exclusively for the voting district in which he lived. The group members decided to become a private, nonprofit organization and seek funds from the Law Enforcement Assistance Agency (LEAA) of the U.S. Department of Justice to pay for a professional director and full-time staff. They replicated the federally funded and politically connected Atlanta NJC and named their center, which began a few months after CMS, the Makiki Neighborhood Justice Center.

The focus of this chapter is on CMS. However, some comparative data will be presented to evaluate the success of the democratically organized and student-administered NJC.

CREATION OF THE COMMUNITY MEDIATION SERVICE

The office staff of CMS was composed exclusively of university faculty and students who volunteered their services for approximately fifteen hours per week. At the outset, some of the staff were trained mediators; some who did not receive mediation training did the work out of interest or in the spirit of innovation and public interest. A particularly unique feature of CMS compared to other models studied was the composition and operation of the board of directors. The staff and mediators became the NJC's board of directors, with each person having an equal vote in establishing policies on all issues. Because no one received any monetary remuneration for their services, it is believed that this democratic feature of the volunteer organization kept CMS running, growing, and healthy. Rather than taking orders from the community leaders, politicians, and experts who comprise the boards of many centers in the United States, the undergraduate students, faculty, and community volunteers made the decisions of CMS. At the outset, students working for CMS did not gain academic credit, yet they gained invaluable experience and exercised considerable clout in serving as voting members of the CMS board of directors.

Under the guidance of board policy, CMS developed a case referral system that at first relied on the city prosecutor's office. The caseload, however, also consisted of referrals from various county, state, and federal (military) agencies. CMS also conducted a community outreach program that generated cases from the community and private organizations. The CMS staff designed and distributed pamphlets, produced radio advertisements, made organizational presentations, and held press conferences to get the word out about their free services.

CMS utilized existing office space, telephones, computers, files, and other office materials at the Department of Political Science for recordkeeping, intake, and follow-up. The mediations, however, were set up in various public and private facilities across the island—such as YWCAs, community centers, and libraries—for the convenience of the parties involved in the conflict. The major operating cost of the center, which the political science department absorbed, was for mailing. Private individuals and a city agency serviced by the center contributed the cost of printing brochures and pamphlets.

MAJOR POLICIES OF THE CMS BOARD OF DIRECTORS

After receiving mediation training and experience in mediating cases, the CMS board of directors held regular meetings to establish policies of the center. Responsibilities for agenda setting and chairing of board meetings were rotated among the members of the board, with undergraduates often assuming those responsibilities with great success. Following are some of the major policies adopted after considerable discussion.

Three-Person Mediation Panel

In order to provide the CMS mediators with more opportunities for role play, the trainer placed them on three-person panels. As it turned out, the mediators discovered several advantages in working as a tribunal rather than as solitary peacemakers. First, with the great ethnic diversity in Hawaii and frequent instances of racial hostility between disputing parties, it was believed to be easier to obtain the trust of the disputants when mediators reflected the ethnic mixture of the parties in conflict. Second, CMS found it helpful to work with a mediator of another ethnic background. Jargon could be handled better when unfamiliar customs and mores were explained during the private caucuses of the mediation panel. Third, by working on a panel, the mediators appreciated support from one another. When it appeared that the mediation was going nowhere or a line of questioning had taken the wrong turn or one of the disputants was suspicious of one of the mediators, another mediator could ease in and change the direction of the process. This helped relieve the pressure a lone mediator feels in a hostile environment. The panel also helped lessen tension afterward to help each mediator "wind down."

However, the most important reason for using the panel method for a university-based NJC is its *educational* value, which takes several forms. Obviously, there is the continual learning process that occurs in working with others. One learns how to handle certain situations by observing other mediators. After each hearing the mediators got together to discuss the case, to analyze how the agreement was reached, what seemed to work and what did not, and to think how similar situations might be handled in the future. Best of all, it permitted undergraduate students the rare opportunity of working as equals with faculty and adult members of the community in a project that pioneered the way for citizen mediation in a large urban area.

However, the panel policy also had a few inherent problems. Scheduling difficulties were created by the necessity of finding three mediators who reflected the ethnicity, sex, and age of the disputants and who could mediate at the same time. This, however, was never a serious problem even though mediators were sometimes given only a few hours notice before a hearing. It also led our board of directors to permit the use of two-mediator panels, which often worked quite well.

Personality differences among mediators sometimes posed problems, but these proved to be minor, and some teams just did not work as well as others. All in all, though, most mediators felt the panel method worked best for both the disputants and the mediators and no one asked to mediate independently.

Closed Hearings: Strict Confidentiality

Since the concept of the mediation center was originally set up to be a community-based model, there was considerable sentiment that the mediations should be open to the public, so that disputes would be less narrowly defined and the problems of the community could be dealt with in an open forum. However, when it became clear that most of the cases in the center involved personal, intimate disputes between two parties, it was decided that the hearings would be limited to the disputants and members of the CMS staff.

Along with the decision to have closed hearings, the CMS board of directors decided that the proceedings would be confidential and the only records kept would be copies of the signed agreements, if agreement was reached. The policy on confidentiality was so strong that it required mediators to tear up their notes as soon as the mediation session was over.

Hearings Held in the Community

While there was adequate space at the university to hold mediation hearings, it was decided that mediations would not be held there. First, colleges and universities intimidate many of the people in the community CMS wished to serve. Second, since the university was at least an hour's drive from some of the poorer sections of the island and parking at the university was a problem, the CMS board decided to go out into the community. This provided no great hardship on the mediators since they came from all areas of the community.

Free Services

The board of directors agreed that services should be free to those who needed them. All mediators volunteered their services. There was some debate over whether or not one should be reimbursed for travel expense, but it was decided that the costs involved were minimal and affordable by the individual mediators.

Case Criteria: Civil and Criminal Cases

The most controversial issue the mediators dealt with was case criteria. Several mediators soon had a reluctance to handle certain types of cases. One mediator felt that no family disputes should be handled, particularly those that involved child or spouse abuse. Another did not want to accept cases involving collection on bad checks. Several mediators were concerned about handling cases that involved any form of violence. A major dispute among mediators arose over the issue of handling cases in which there was a great power differential between the parties.

After debating the pros and cons of accepting various cases, the board of directors decided that the overriding principles involved in accepting a case would be: (1) the existence of an ongoing relationship between the parties and (2) agreement among all disputants to try mediation. Each mediator had the option to refuse to hear a case. As it turned out, most mediators dropped their reservations about hearing certain cases and accepted the staff's judgment (usually that of an undergraduate student) about whether or not a case was suitable for mediation.

The board met monthly to add to or change policies and to discuss ideas and problems mediators had during the month. No decision could be made without a quorum present, which was never a problem. Most mediators maintained a very high level of enthusiasm and activity in the pilot project.

THE CURRICULUM OF THE NEIGHBORHOOD JUSTICE CENTER

For the first few months of its existence, CMS operated out of the university and was staffed by students and faculty. It was supported by the political science department, but it was not an official project with a director and funded by the university. It was not an institute or a clinic. It was just an NJC based in a university office that was financially subsidized by the personal funds of some of the political science faculty. No one received payment for work in the center. The initial training cost a few thousand dollars and brochures cost a few hundred dollars more, all of which came from faculty contributions.

CMS served as a useful laboratory for the researching of alternative dispute resolution techniques, community building, and transformed governance. As lessons were learned, new hypotheses arose to be tested or ideas transformed into experiments. It was a synergistic center that meshed theory with practice. Fortunately, one of the survivors of the vast change in university curricula of the 1960s at the University of Hawaii was the existence of such courses as independent studies, practicums, and internships. As a result, CMS developed a mutually beneficial training process for staff and mediators that allowed undergraduate students, under the supervision of faculty, to obtain academic credit by serving as apprentices at CMS. Students within the political science department were allowed to take up to three semester courses (three credit hours each) in practical coursework. Faculty working with CMS developed a number of options for students. The on-campus internship program allowed students to sign up for independent study or as interns to work in the university-based NJC. Depending on their particular interests or circumstances, students could sign up for three to nine semester hours of credit in practicums or independent study courses.

All students who signed up for such classes, however, had to do required reading and attend classes. The classes often served as "staff" meetings in which to discuss various aspects of the readings, particularly as they related to the worldwide mediation situation. Slowly, the students learned the office work and all facets and phases of CMS. If they were able to complete and master all components of the process, known as the "apprenticeship model," they became certified CMS mediators and members of the board of directors.

THE APPRENTICESHIP MODEL

The faculty and CMS board of directors designed an apprenticeship model that had four phases.

Phase 1

Students were required to read research materials on mediation and NJCs. Apprentices also read literature on how mediation hearings differ from courtroom hearings. Articles and books written by anthropologists, lawyers, sociologists, psychologists, political scientists, and community leaders provided the necessary background for apprentices to move on to the next phase.

Phase 2

Students moved into office work. After becoming familiar with the office manual describing the policies and procedures at CMS, the apprentices began work under the guidance of a CMS director (student, faculty, or community mediator). They learned and practiced all aspects of the office work and had to work on four cases using any combination of the following tasks before moving on to the third phase: arranging a mediation, conducting a telephone conciliation, and/or patching up a broken agreement.

Phase 3

This phase involved simulation and observation of actual mediations. After apprentices read a manual on mediation techniques, they had to participate as mediators on at least two simulation panels. The Department of Sociology had a small-group lab with a one-way window. Faculty from the political science and sociology departments, who served on CMS board of directors, developed and supervised the simulations.

Initially, apprentices had to participate in two simulations before any observations of real mediations could take place. Later, however, they observed a mediation after only one simulation. Observation often served as a useful teaching devise to emphasize the points made during the critique of the simulation. Students still had to participate in at least two simulations before they observed two mediations and receive the approval of one of the simulation instructors before they moved to the next phase.

Phase 4

The final phase involved the students sitting in on actual mediation panels as extra mediators. For purposes of the mediation, apprentices acted as full-fledged mediators, sharing equally in the explanation of the mediation and in the questioning of the disputants. After each mediation, the mediators and an apprentice held a discussion to evaluate the process and behavior of those involved in the mediation. Not only did these discussions involve a critique of the apprentice's behavior, but the apprentice also questioned the mediators about why certain questions were asked or why sessions were handled in particular ways. Once an apprentice received the approval of five CMS mediators (which was possible only after two mediations), he or she was certified by the CMS board of directors as a trained mediator and automatically became a member of the board.

After completing the CMS apprenticeship, the student mediator had a much more comprehensive knowledge of all aspects of the NJC than did the original mediators. Because they had functioned as staff as well as mediators, they were able to develop proposals and projects that took into consideration the needs, limitations, and expertise of both the staff and mediators. They developed a better understanding and appreciation of the crucial and effective role played by the staff in the mediation center. They acquired a keen, empirically based comprehension of a process and set of techniques that are extremely effective in conflict resolution at both individual and group levels. The apprenticeship training combined studies in psychology, sociology, anthropology, law, and political science that analyzed techniques incorporated into the CMS model of conflict resolution.

ADVANTAGES OF THE UNIVERSITY-BASED NEIGHBORHOOD JUSTICE CENTERS

Availability of University Resources

Adding an NJC to the university curriculum brings a cornucopia of economic, social, and educational benefits. As in the case of CMS, universities often have resources that can be utilized by the mediation center without much additional cost, such as office space, telephones, typewriters, computers, and office equipment. CMS shared space with a statewide public opinion polling project that was operating out of the political science department. Utilization of existing space and equipment, however, needs the support of colleagues and university administrators. It is important that they see merit in the project and at least lend moral support. They can also publicize its success in terms of demonstrating how the university is continuing to improve its outreach programs.

Faculty and Student Staffing

The staff of CMS was composed largely of students who volunteered their services and/or received academic credit. After an initial expense of providing training for mediators, the operating expenses of a university-based NJC are considerably lower than court or court "annexed" programs with relatively high-paid directors and associate directors. The salaries of the "executive directors" were those of professors in the capacity as teachers, not administrators. Costs of CMS did not begin to reach what were described as the "relatively modest budgets" of the Columbus, Ohio, and Rochester, New York, centers with operating costs in 1977 of $43,000 and $65,000, respectively (McGillis 1978:7).

Independence from Funding Source Constraints

In 1996 dollars, the annual cost of a program the size of CMS would be approximately $300,000 for other models. A university-based program similar to CMS would cost next to nothing—given the curriculum base of the project.

The low-cost, curriculum-based operation provides an independence from funding sources that may inhibit experimentation or may emphasize priorities not chosen by those involved in administering the program. It shifts the time and energy of the executive director into improving the services offered by the center or into generating research. It is often the case that executive directors spend the bulk of their time scrounging around for funding. But, as long as interest and need exist, the NJC can exist because it relies primarily on the existence of the supportive university curriculum, not external funding.

Combining Theory and Practice

In addition to the economic factor and independence that favor establishment of NJCs within universities, there is an ever-increasing need for universities to wed theory and practice. A frequent criticism made of universities and academics is that they are too theoretical, too critical, too removed from reality, and not really interested in the community that pays the bills. Politicians and business and community leaders often ignore the recommendations and suggestions made by university professors whom they believe live in ivory towers conducting (from their perspective) meaningless studies.

University Assistance to the Community

One way that colleges and universities may lessen the distance between them and their surrounding communities is to play a part in the political conversion to less government bureaucracy and greater community self-sufficiency. By offering a practical program that is based in sound theory, the university can provide a continual flow of mediators into the community who can utilize their peacemaking skills in all sorts of personal and organizational settings. Particularly at a time when social tension and conflict seem sure to rise in the future, this service from a university curriculum can only bring smiles to the faces of people in the community who primarily would only frown at the mention of academia.

Student Internships to Learn and Apply Useful Skills

CMS met the demands of students who wanted to acquire social, commercial, personal, and political skills. Students working under the guidance of faculty developed the referral system; conducted the public relations; became liaisons with the community and legal and military agencies; designed the CMS office forms and procedures; and successfully mediated many agreements over the telephone as well as in actual hearings. Their motivation level remained high. Students contributed hours of volunteer work in addition to the course requirements. When CMS subsequently became the model for a city-sponsored community mediation program, four of the students involved in the CMS program from the outset wrote a manual on office procedures and were hired to help train the workers who were to run the city centers.

Source for Ongoing Research and Experimentation

Whether mediation training is provided free or for a fee, it represents an important contribution that can be made through the resources of the university. It needs the compilation of knowledge and expertise of sociologists, psychologists, political scientists, and communication specialists. Not only does the university have the data and research available for training, but its faculty is experienced in teaching and evaluating. It is unfortunate that these resources available at universities have not been utilized more by NJCs across the country, particularly when the cost of bringing in outside consultants/trainers is high.

COMMUNITY MEDIATION SERVICE'S SUCCESS

This social and academic experiment would be worthless if the curriculum-based, university-headquartered NJC failed to produce *results*. The data provided in Tables 5.1 and 5.2 shows that the unique combination of students, faculty, and community volunteers produced the successful resolution of numerous conflicts in the community via democratic processes and techniques. Table 5.1 presents data on the CMS caseload: number of cases entering the office and the referral sources. Table 5.2 presents follow-up survey results of disputants who had their cases successfully resolved at CMS.

After nearly a year of operation, CMS conducted an analysis of the type of cases referred to them and how the cases were resolved. Table 5.1 reports this breakdown. Most of the 227 referrals to the center came from the prosecutor's office (46 percent). However, the success of the public relations program and community outreach was obvious, with nearly a third of the cases coming from self-referrals (18 percent) and community agencies (11 percent). The remaining cases were referred by Legal Aid (9 percent), family court (6 percent), and the Neighborhood Commission (6 percent), a county department that served as a lightning rod for neighborhood disputes. The commission later established its own mediation service and hired CMS faculty and students to train volunteers and staff. CMS also worked hard to attract cases from military agencies. In Hawaii, service personnel get involved in many disputes with local residents and community mediation provided a welcome service.

Table 5.1
Community Mediation Service Cases During First Nine Months of
Operation

Nature of Dispute (N=227)	# of Cases	Percent
Domestic: Visitation	11	5%
Domestic: Child Support	4	2%
Domestic: Family Dispute	29	13%
Neighbor Dispute	55	24%
Friend/ex-Friend Dispute	58	25%
Landlord-Tenant	29	13%
Consumer Merchant	36	16%
Employer-Employee	5	2%

Origin of Case (N=227)	# of Cases	Percent
Family Court	13	6%
Prosecutor's Office	104	46%
Community Agencies	25	11%
Self-Referrals	41	18%
Legal Aid	20	9%
Military	11	5%
Neighborhood Commission	13	6%

Resolution of Case (Cases Closed) (N=211)	# of Cases	Percent
Failed to Arrange/ Screened-out	93	44%
Hearing Set/No-Show	8	4%
Hearing Held/No Agreement	4	2%
Hearing Held/Agreement Reached	38	18%
Telephone Conciliation	38	18%
Parties Reach Agreement Themselves	30	14%

Table 5.2
Community Mediation Service Follow-Up Survey Results

1.	How satisfied were you with the agreement reached at the CMS mediation hearing you participated in? __46%__ very satisfied __46%__ satisfied __0__ unsatisfied __8%__ very unsatisfied
2.	To what extent has the other party kept to the terms of the agreement? __50%__ completely __42%__ satisfactorily __6%__ not too well __2%__ broken it
3.	In your opinion, is the problem which resulted in the complaint resolved? __89%__ yes, totally resolved __13%__ the problem is only partially resolved __0__ the problem still exists

4.	If you have future problems resulting in disputes of a similar nature, what would you do? __0__ I would try and ignore it and do nothing. __6%__ I would try to work it out myself. __71%__ I would file a complaint with CMS. __17%__ I would file a complaint in court or seek a lawyer. __6%__ Other (Specify)..
	Now, if you don't mind, we'd like to ask just a few questions about our mediation process to help us improve it as much as possible.
5.	If you had a choice, how many mediators would you have preferred to hear your case? __30%__ one __40%__ two __30%__ three __0__ more than three

Table 5.2 (continued)

6.	How would you describe the attitude of your mediators?
	_100%_ very open-minded ___ open-minded ___ somewhat biased ___ very biased
7.	How helpful were the mediators to you?
	_69%_ very helpful _23%_ helpful _8%_ not too helpful _0_ made matters worse

Half of the cases referred to the center involved either disputes between friends or disputes between neighbors, the cases that CMS had always felt would be best served by mediation centers. The two categories of cases that produced considerable debate when the board was determining case criteria were domestic disputes (quarrels among family members, child support, and visitation rights conflicts) and consumer-merchant disputes, which comprised nearly one-third of all cases referred to the center. The remainder involved either landlord-tenant or employer-employee disputes.

The staff screened out over 40 percent of the cases referred to CMS because there was no ongoing relationship between the parties or one of the parties was unwilling to mediate. However, some form of agreement was reached in 50 percent of the cases coming into CMS either by the parties reaching an agreement themselves (14%), telephone conciliation conducted by a staff member (18%), or mediation through a successful session (18%). The rate of success in reaching agreements at the mediation sessions, once they were held, was 90 percent. This high success rate was due to a combination of factors: the staff's skill in explaining the mediation process to the parties, the willingness of the parties to compromise, and the skills of the mediators in helping the parties communicate and resolve their differences.

The staff at CMS, under the guidance of the board, designed a questionnaire to determine how effective the program was in helping individuals resolve their disputes. CMS wanted to obtain feedback from those utilizing its services to help evaluate its policies and procedures and to make them as responsive as possible to the needs of the community. Follow-up surveys were conducted by the staff one month after the mediation was held and again two months later.

After more than nine months of operation, follow-up data was compiled on forty-five cases that CMS had resolved and in which they were able to contact the parties involved. The data in Table 5.2 is based on ninety interviews. Not only were 92 percent of the respondents either very satisfied with the mediation hearing, but 89 percent said the problem was totally resolved and none said the problem still existed. In addition, 71 percent said they would file a complaint with CMS in the future if they had problems resulting in disputes of a similar nature.

These figures compare favorably with data from heavily funded NJCs in Atlanta, Kansas City, and Los Angeles. Composite data from three centers representing responses from over one thousand disputants showed: 84 percent were satisfied with the mediation; and 73 percent state they would return to the NJC for similar problems in the future (McGillis 1978:5). In evaluating CMS mediators, 100 percent of the respondents stated that the mediators were very open-minded, and 92 percent said the mediators were helpful. It appeared that the CMS panel method made some difference to the disputants: 40 percent preferred two mediators; 30 percent wanted one; 30 percent wanted three; and none preferred more than three.

The results of the survey had a very positive impact on the mediators and spurred a new burst of energy in the midst of a difficult year of learning, much of which came by trial and error. It convinced the interns, staff, and mediators that their services were, indeed, needed and appreciated.

PROSPECTS FOR THE FUTURE

The faculty who envisioned CMS and funded the original training of mediators established the program as a prototype to demonstrate the capability of average citizens to learn mediation skills and to use those skills to serve as conflict resolvers in their communities and in their personal lives. Grounded in the philosophy of democratic community, they sought to train others to take these citizen-empowerment services into their own neighborhoods. After a year of operation, the city and county of Honolulu received a federal grant to develop a network of mediation centers throughout the county. They hired CMS faculty and students to train their staff and volunteer mediators.

The Makiki Neighborhood Justice Center, the lawyer-led splinter group, reversed its original plan to stay local and handle no family disputes. It began to mediate islandwide and to handle the wide array of cases that CMS had chosen to handle from the outset. They sought and received substantial federal funding to hire a professional director, two associate directors, and two clerical workers. With their economically prominent and politically connected board of directors, they were able to obtain state funding when the federal funds ran out.

Since the CMS faculty funders and researchers had never envisioned an ongoing center on campus, but merely a demonstration project, when their one-year plan was completed with city-run mediation centers sprouting up around the island, they arranged internships for the university students in the off-campus centers. The students, with advising from faculty, then established a mediation service on campus to handle student and faculty problems exclusively.

The off-campus internships proved to be very disappointing to most students. They felt underutilized, subservient, and unwanted. They certainly did not obtain voting rights as members of the board of directors of the NJCs. In evaluation surveys at the conclusion of their internships, they complained extensively about the lack of appreciation they received and the lack of input they had in the centers off campus.

The faculty realized their original vision to have the university contribute to the development of mediation centers around the island beyond their initial expectations. An unanticipated benefit was the manner in which students would assume responsibility and relish the opportunity to contribute their time and expertise to working closely with and helping others. Unfortunately, when they moved into the city-run or professionally run centers, they were treated as blue-collar and pink-collar workers only there to take orders.

Comparative data clearly demonstrates that the faculty-student-community CMS program, which was democratically run, was as successful (if not more so) as the other, heavily funded program in Hawaii. The costs were considerably less and time was spent exclusively on casework and learning about mediation—not on fund-raising and the creation of expensive bureaucracies. And most importantly, the educational advantage of teaching democracy by being democratic was evident and appreciated by both students and faculty.

NOTES

1. For an excellent history of the early development of the NJC movement in the United States, see Daniel McGillis, *Neighborhood Justice Centers* (Washington, D.C.: Government Printing Office, 1978). Cf. Benedict Alper and Lawrence Nichols, *Beyond the Courtroom: Programs in Community Justice and Conflict Resolution* (Lexington, Mass.: Lexington Books, 1981).

2. See Paul Warhaftig, ed., *The Citizen Dispute Resolution Handbook* (Pittsburgh, Pa.: Middle Atlantic Region, American Friends Service Committee, 1977).

REFERENCES

Alper, Benedict and Lawrence Nichols. 1981. *Beyond the Courtroom: Programs in Community Justice and Conflict Resolution.* Lexington, Mass.: Lexington Books.

McGills, Daniel. 1978. *Neighborhood Justice Centers.* Washington, D.C.: Government
    Printing Office.
Warhaftig, Paul, ed. 1977. *The Citizen Dispute Resolution Handbook.* Pittsburgh, Pa.:
    Middle Atlantic Region, American Friends Service Committee.

6

Televote: Interactive, Participatory Polling

Theodore L. Becker

This chapter describes a rather unique experiment in American democracy and an equally original test of experiential education. The lesson: how to enhance citizen participation in a modern representative democracy via an undergraduate political science course.

PUBLIC OPINION AND DEMOCRACY

Theoretically, public opinion is supposed to strongly influence both representative and direct forms of democracy. The theory of representative democracy maintains that the electoral process is the way public opinion decides whether those in power are doing a good enough job to be reelected. If not, public opinion—as manifested through the behavior of a majority of the voters—will remove them from office. Public opinion checks political power and political leaders ignore it at their peril.

Therefore, in modern republics—the usual term for representative democracies or, as they are also called, indirect democracies—those who run for office theoretically use public opinion polling in a wide variety of forms to see what is important to those most likely to show up at the ballot box. They hire expensive political consultants to analyze scientific "snapshots" of public opinion most relevant to their election so as to determine how to shape and style their campaign. Once in office, public opinion polls, particularly those conducted by the mass media, continue to inform them of any changes so that they may respond in some fashion to them. Thus, public opinion polls are a technological recreation of accountability, the key philosophical foundation of the republican form of government. They reveal the "consent of the governed" and/or the lack thereof. Theoretically.

Public opinion has an equally, if not more, significant role to play in direct democracy. In direct democratic forms like initiative, referendum, and town meetings, public opinion—that segment of it that turns out to vote—determines policy, that is, public opinion gets directly transformed into law by the voters. Legislation, in this case, is no longer left to the representatives of the people. It becomes the work of the people themselves.

PROBLEMS WITH THE THEORY

Of course, as with all theories, the reality of public opinion doesn't fit democratic practice so neatly. In fact, the gap between the theory of how public opinion is supposed to work in representative democracies and how it actually works is so great that the theory is often referred to these days as "mythology." Shelves of books over the past decades have demonstrated that public opinion—whether that be determined by scientific samples or by self-selected samples of voters—has little relationship to keeping representatives accountable to the people. Indeed, it is now clear that a huge industry has been constructed to "manufacture" the consent of the governed for the benefit of ruling political, economic, and social elites (Lippmann 1922).

Actually, there are a number of valid reasons given by those in power as to why they pay so little attention to public opinion, particularly that part of it measured by modern opinion survey companies. They note that what passes for public opinion is really nothing more than "off-the-top-of-the-head" reactions to simple, often superficial questions posed by the pollsters. Many studies have revealed that, indeed, such public opinion is based on little information and/or a lot of misinformation. So, legislators and other political leaders discount it as being either (1) an inaccurate reading of public opinion or (2) an accurate measure of the poor quality of the uninformed opinion of scientific samples of the citizenry. In either event, public officials readily dismiss public opinion as worth little other than to give them some idea about which way the wind blows prior to elections. Polls at election time function mainly to uncover the best "buzzwords" to include in thirty-second television campaign ads that attempt to make 50 percent of the voters believe that the candidates will do what that group wants once they are elected or reelected to office.

The truth be told, there is a great deal of evidence to support such a critique of modern public opinion polling techniques. Despite this electoral manipulation, current polling techniques have evolved and improved with time. Public opinion polling for campaign purposes first appeared on the American scene in 1824, with other sporadic attempts at it reappearing throughout the latter part of the nineteenth century and the early part of the twentieth. But it wasn't until George Gallup set up his political survey company in 1935 that public opinion polling became regular, systematic, and independent of the media—a permanent feature of American political life between elections.

However, even as it became a growth industry in the United States, political polling to predict election results suffered through some highly publicized and devastating mistakes, particularly in predicting presidential "horse races." In 1948, all major, national public opinion organizations forecasted a landslide for Thomas Dewey over President Harry S. Truman, but the only avalanche came in the form of heavy criticism and gleeful derision from all quarters after Truman was reelected.

This highly publicized gaffe came about because it was the common practice among pollsters at that time to quit surveying a few days before the actual election. Contemporary pollsters continue to ask questions right up to election day. They even intercept people coming out of the voting booths to see if their preelection day forecasts hit the target. Because of this and other corrections that are constantly being made, modern pollsters are pretty accurate in predicting electoral results.

Using survey techniques to gauge public opinion on complex issues of policy, though, is quite another matter. All modern issue polling, no matter how scientific the sample and how careful the design of the questions, still fails to provide much—if any—relevant information and/or expert opinion. Moreover, the reply sought is immediate, no matter what the person might be doing or thinking at the moment. Isn't adequate information about the subject and the time to think about it the essence of coming to a sound judgment on a policy? We expect our elected officials to take some time to grasp an issue and consider its implications and consequences, and we expect them to marshal at least some data while considering various sides of an issue. Small wonder that elected officials are quick to disparage the opinion of citizens who have had no opportunity to do the same.

Of course, pollsters are not the only sources of poorly informed public opinion. There are many manufacturers of public mis- and noninformation on issues, including the electronic media, the newspapers, and even elected officials themselves. A pioneer in public opinion polling was asked in the early 1960s what kind of job he thought the press was doing in furnishing the American people the information needed by an attentive public to form intelligent opinions on major issues. He responded that the mass media concentrated too much on spot news reporting instead of providing more information on the major issues, elaborating on this background, and being more thoughtful and interesting.

The situation is even worse now, more than three decades since Gallup made his observation. The reason for this is obvious enough. Study after study indicates that over 70 percent of the American people get all or most of their news and information on politics from television—a medium notorious for its poor memory and minuscule attention span. Furthermore, today's issues seem ever more complex, requiring even more information and more time for reflection. Thus, American public opinion is probably in a more precarious situation today than ever before. The public wants and needs to be included in the policy-making process, but public opinion pollsters continue to utilize the outdated methods that produce a poor quality of public opinion based mostly on superficial TV reportage.

THE TELEVOTE METHOD OF POLLING AS A SOLUTION TO THE PROBLEM

Over the past twenty years, there have been a series of experiments in California, Hawaii, and New Zealand known as "the Televote experiments." Televote, a generic term, means voting-by-telecommunications (telephone, computer, and so forth.). However, as a method of public opinion polling, it is highly innovative and responsive to many of the criticisms about polling.

Televote differs from conventional polling in that it provides respondents with a dollop of undisputed information about an issue, several balanced arguments for and against various aspects of proposed solutions, and a wide array of options. It also yields ample time for the respondents to think about the problem or issue and encourages them to discuss it with as many friends, family members, coworkers, or experts as they desire. Dr. Vincent Campbell, who invented this method of polling under a National Science Foundation grant in 1974 put it like this: "If citizen opinions are to have beneficial effect on government decisions, they should be well-informed and thoughtful. The Televote system informs people by giving them summaries of information relevant to the issues, easy access to more detailed information, and time to think the whole matter over before deciding" (Campbell 1975: 5).

Campbell worked with the board of education of San Jose, California, the local Parent-Teacher Association, and some concerned citizens to set up an agenda of what were the most pressing educational issues facing the city. This research gathered information relevant to these issues that Campbell then disseminated to the general public through radio, television, and newspapers. In addition, Campbell prepared a ballot and citizens were invited to participate in the project by registering to vote. Upon registration, they were given a personal identification number that they had to dial in before their vote would be counted. Prior to the balloting on each issue, the Televoters received a packet of information in the mail about the issue under consideration. An automated computer program tallied the votes of those Televoters who telephoned in their responses. Within a few days, the results of each of the nine San Jose Televotes were mailed by the Televote staff to the board of education, to the PTA, and to the media.

How successful was this initial Televote poll experiment? The results were mixed. The process produced a highly biased sample of Televoters, perhaps the major flaw. As in most real referenda, those who participated did not represent the entire spectrum of the population. This new method of gathering public opinion skewed the demographics on a number of major variables. In addition, the process was quite expensive, costing $30,000 in 1974. Thus, it was clear that some drastic changes had to be made in the Televote method devised by Campbell to make it an improvement on conventional polling.

IMPROVING THE TELEVOTE METHOD OF POLLING

A team of political scientists at the University of Hawaii heard about the Televote experiment in 1977 and liked its design and some of its results. The team saw an opportunity to replicate and improve Campbell's work. Hawaii was just about ready to embark on a constitutional convention, scheduled for the summer of 1978, that had some extremely important and complex issues on the agenda: initiative and referendum, the method of appointing judges, nuclear power, protection of the environment, and so forth.

The group believed that Televoting would be ideal for such complicated issues. The citizenry needed some basic information and some time to think about it. What other method of polling could provide those essential elements? On the other hand, there were pressing problems. How could the huge bias in the sample be eliminated? Who would pay for the most expensive part of such a polling system, that is, the Televote staff? Was there some way to pare the budget? After thinking the problems through, the Hawaii Televote group found some answers.

First, the group changed the method of recruiting the Televoters. Instead of letting the Televoters choose themselves, the new Televote method utilized the scientific polling method of telephone random-digit dialing. Upon reaching a citizen by phone, the Televote representative asked if he or she would be willing to receive a Televote information brochure in the mail, to read it, to take the time to discuss it with friends, family, and so forth, to answer the questions on the brochure, and then to call back with an opinion. If the citizen agreed to all this, he or she would be signed up and a brochure would be mailed.

The next problem was to get enough Televoters to follow through on this so that the group wouldn't still end up with a highly biased sample. Early on in the process, we found that this was indeed a problem, that is, only a small percentage were actually calling in their votes. As a result, we needed the Televote staff to do a great deal of telephoning, reminding the Televoters of their promise to cooperate, and, many times, getting them to answer the Televote questions while we had them on the line.

The final problem was money—how to get a Televote staff to do this without any funding. Where would we get the money for mailing out the brochures? How were we going to pay for the telephone bills? Where would we get money to rent an office? The answers were obvious as we pondered the questions in the offices of the Department of Political Science. The key was to come up with the right question: Why not make Televote into a university course?

TELEVOTE AS EXPERIENTIAL EDUCATION IN MODERN DEMOCRACY

Once the idea hit the Televote team, everything began falling into place. We would add a practicum or internship course into our curriculum that specified Televote as the practical experience. What's the difference whether or not the experience takes place inside or outside the university, particularly if the relationship is with the outside community? In terms of program, it could fit within the broad spectrum allowed under the rubric American government, and if it would be utilized by a particular agency of government, like the Department of Health, it could readily be an internship within a public administration program.

For starters, the course would touch on democratic theory and the fundamentals of American government, the legislative process, and public administration. Some of the readings would focus on the plethora of modern criticism of this theory and institutional analysis. Criticism that pointed out low citizen participation, efforts to increase it, and the inadequacies of public opinion polling, would be excellent background.

After a short course in the history and procedures of modern public opinion polling in America, the students would be introduced to the Televote process developed by Campbell and to its shortcomings. At that point, the Televote team would introduce its innovations and the class would be ready to become the Televote staff.

With agreement from the department chair, the Televote office would be ready for action. What was needed was a telephone bank and mailing privileges. The main office telephone system could be used as the telephone bank, particularly since all the Televoter recruiting and interaction would be limited to evenings and weekends. These are the best times to reach a representative sample of the population as they are the best times to reach the American work force. The office phones of one or two faculty members could be utilized to recruit and interact with other citizens during ordinary working hours in order to recruit those citizens who work evenings and weekends. Random-digit dialing lists can be purchased from polling companies for a modest sum and the mailing privileges of the university can be used for such educational purposes. Designing and printing the Televote brochure, while somewhat costly in the late 1970s, is far easier today since the advent of desktop publishing programs.

Once these logistical curriculum matters are taken care of and the material support system is in place, the Televote class must be converted into the Televote staff. By the time they have become fully acquainted with the problems in modern American democracy, most are highly motivated to give the revised Televote system the old college try.

ORGANIZING AND SUPERVISING THE TELEVOTE STAFF

Organizing and running a Televote out of the curriculum and employing students who have had no experience at conducting even an ordinary public opinion poll is not easily done. However, if there are an adequate number of students enrolled in the course (twelve to fifteen) and they are organized into groups, the entire operation can be run smoothly and professionally.

The Agenda-Setting Process

The initial function of the staff is to determine what issue will serve as the focus of the Televote. The students must understand that setting the agenda for the process is not something to be taken lightly because they may subsequently take a lot of flak for these early decisions. Some critics are likely to claim, for example, that the Televote staff—if it acts capriciously in selecting the subject of the Televote—is merely showing its bias and imitating what elite-controlled or elite-influenced survey companies and/or legislators are criticized for doing, that is, having a "hidden agenda."

One method of setting the agenda involves determining what are the most important issues in the minds of the public. A content analysis of recent newspapers, that is, the articles, the editorials and, of course, the letters to the editors, offers some evidence of issues. If there were a recent political campaign, the literature of the candidates could be examined as well. The staff could be more or less "scientific" about setting the agenda. In Hawaii, it was pretty obvious from these written materials what issues should be subjects of the Hawaii Televotes.

However, we also tried another method that proved to be quite successful. We asked a random sample of Televoters and culled from that what we called the public agenda. This was done by compiling a long list of issues from the newspapers and campaign flyers. We put them into a brochure and used the Televote method on a random sample of citizens, asking them to come up with their own list of priorities. The public's agenda then dictated the next two substantive Televotes we conducted. The Televote staff learned a number of democratic lessons through this process. First, we got an excellent response from the public. It was easy to sign up Televoters for this process. This indicated that citizens were as willing, if not more willing, to think about and give their opinions on agenda setting as they had been on making policy decisions or deciding constitutional issues.

Second, much as the critics had warned, the Televote staff view on the public's agenda was wrong. The random sample of Televoters came up with different priorities than the Televote staff had expected. Third, despite our care in the entire process and improved sample demographics, the media were highly skeptical of the results. They thought they had a better idea of what was important to the public than did a highly representative sample of over four hundred Televoters. Nevertheless, one of the major networks used the Televote results as the basis for a five-day series of issue-oriented news shows the following week. The agenda-setting process provided the Televoting team an excellent experiential education about how the public and elites may well think differently about what are the most pressing issues of the day.

The Research Committee-of-the-Whole

Once the staff and/or public has selected the Televote topic, the next major step is to do the background research on it. This intensive process requires a great deal of work in a short amount of time. So, the entire staff (class) becomes the Televote research department. Some of the staff assigns itself to the library or computer (Internet) research work. Realizing that the Televote brochure is not going to be book length, they must choose only some basic facts that are completely undisputed. For example, if the topic was initiative and referendum, they needed to find out how many states had them, when they began doing them, what percentage of them are passed, and other similar facts. The general idea is not to overwhelm the Televoters with data, but to supply enough basic information to educate them in the fundamentals and to stimulate their thinking and talking about the issue. Today computer research could enable the staff to provide further information upon request of the Televoters during later stages in the process.

The Televote research staff also obtains and describes the pro and con arguments of advocates of two or more positions on the issue under consideration, which can be done mostly through newspaper content analysis. However, experts or proponents of various viewpoints should agree with the description of their positions in the Televote brochure. Thus, once the major opposing arguments are written and the staff agrees to them, then the prominent advocates of both or multiple sides of the issues are asked to edit and verify the accuracy of the descriptions of their statements.

A multitude of important lessons emerge in this part of the Televote course/process. First, students learn to do basic research on public issues via the library or computer databases. Second, they learn to work together—to collaborate and cooperate—with one another as researchers and analysts. Third, they meet with political and community leaders in the role of facilitators in order to work out the best wording in the pro and con argument section of the Televote—also playing an important public relations role for Televote in the process.

The final stage of the research process comes when professional pollsters are invited to attend the Televote staff meeting at which the final product is put together and published. The pollsters, who are provided copies of the draft prior to their arrival, then pepper the staff with questions about the data, the wording, and any biases they detect. This gives the staff an opportunity to be criticized by experts and, once they have made necessary changes that are satisfactory to the professionals, gives them a good deal of confidence in the final product.

Meanwhile, the participating faculty member or members have been working with illustrators, a printing company, and a survey company to come up with the final design of the brochure and to procure the random-digit dialing lists. The Televote survey process is about to begin.

The Interactive Polling Process

The Televote polling process, in contradiction to all other conventional public opinion survey processes, is highly interactive. This puts a great deal of work and pressure on the Televote staff as salespersons, interviewers, and educators. In addition, because of the heavy workload required, the staff must learn to work together very closely in a high-pressure situation.

Right from the start, the Televote staff is well aware that the key to success is to get a high percentage of the citizens reached by phone to sign up for the process. At least 50 percent of those contacted need to be recruited and about 75 percent of them need to vote in order to get within, or very close to, the +/− 5 percent on each demographic variable. So learning how to be a good telemarketer is a quintessential aspect of the project.

Once again, everyone in the class, including the professors, are part of the Televote interview team, remaining there until the required number of Televoters answers the survey. The minimum quota is that number theoretically required for a +/− 5 percent margin of error, or approximately 380 Televoters. This callout—recruitment—and callback—reminding the Televoters of their commitment to read the Televote, discuss it, and vote on it—period takes between two and three weeks. Because of the number of callbacks that are usually necessary, an elaborate system of recordkeeping is needed, and in order to maintain some quality control, close supervision is also required.

Once again, numerous and impressive democratic lessons emerge from this stage of the Televote. First, the students learn the importance of collaborating as a team, a team that is dedicated to improving the quality of public participation in the political process. Second, they learn that citizens in all walks of life are not only willing, but also eager to take some time out of their busy and sometimes troubled lives to work on this project for no material reward. Third, they discover that only a very few of those who must be recalled numerous times get angry and/or drop out. Fourth, they find out, when asking all those who complete the Televote whether they would like to participate in the project again in the future, that fully 90 percent of them—even those who have been recalled a dozen times—say they would.

Being a Televote staff interviewer, then, is a superb lesson in participatory democracy for the students through their own personal experience. It is a rebuke to those in power who repeat their tired refrain that the public is apathetic and disinterested in politics and would never take the time and trouble necessary to study the complicated issues that legislators must resolve. Televote interviewers learn firsthand just how wrong this argument is and understand from an intense personal engagement how grateful many citizens are to be invited to be Televoters—even though most of them are highly skeptical that anyone in government will care anything about what the results of the Televote will be. They are satisfied enough when they are told that the results will be broadcast on radio and television and will appear in one of the newspapers in their town, city, or state. In other words, it is just as, or more, important for citizens to have a say about agendas and issues after informed deliberation as it is for them to believe that those in power care about and/or would act on what they have said.

The Public Relations Committee

As the Televote callback process is winding down, some of the interview staff becomes the public relations committee. This committee takes the substantive and demographic information from the records—which can be constantly updated on the computer system—and analyzes the results. Meeting as a staff, committee members decide how to refine this information into a short news release. They draft a preliminary version of the release and present it at a full Televote staff meeting for criticism, revision, and editing, then writing the final version.

Next, the public relations committee distributes a copy of the news release to all media outlets in the city, state, and country by mail or fax. At the same time, they telephone key people in the major newspapers and television and radio stations to tell them that they will have a press conference the next day to discuss the news release. Finally, the committee mails a copy of the press release to all important people in the community who have an interest in this particular issue, including legislators, administrators, and community leaders.

Before the time of the actual press conference, the rest of the Televote staff grills the committee members on various questions concerning the theory and methodology of the Televote process, the results, and what they think the government will do with the results. This is a sort of "dress rehearsal" for the real thing, which is usually attended by a fair representation of the press.

The lessons learned from this experience are dramatic and rewarding. For example, the students on the committee learn the rudiments of the public relations game—in terms of how to produce a news release, conduct a press conference, and how to deal with various members of the mass media, from the irremediably cynical to the most open-minded. The way mass media representatives relate to surveys gives students an inside view of the attitudes and modus vivendi of the media as participants in contemporary democratic practice. In a very real sense, the students on the committee learn to play a novel and difficult role as public proponents of innovation and participatory democracy. At the same time, they are dispassionate reporters of the state of public opinion on important topics. As such, they also gain valuable insights into the range of attitudes and opinions in the media on these subjects. Finally, once again, the students are thrust into teamwork—this time under the glare of the white-hot television lights.

Establishing a Network at a State or National Level

The New Zealand Televote in 1981 replicated Televote as a college course at a national level. Three universities—Christchurch College, Victoria University of Wellington, and Auckland University—wove together a Televote network that connected them in different parts of the country. Each professor used a similar syllabus and mode of operation and worked together via the mail and telephone. This was prior to the advent of electronic mail and fax machines. The country was divided into regions—south, central, and north—which were serviced by the Televote staff (students) in each part of the country.

Collating the data and preparing the press release and conference was done at the central location. Thus, the students at Victoria University of Wellington were the only ones to be on the public relations committee. The students at the other universities participated in all other parts of the process and in their educational benefits, for example, learning the theoretical material and applying it through all the other experiences in the Televoting process. The entire project was done on a shoestring budget of less than $10,000 (U.S.).

The faculty of the project discussed it and agreed that the students were completely engaged by the process, giving it high evaluations as experiential education. This brings us to evaluating Televote—both as an exercise in experiential education at the college level and as a new method of interactive polling facilitated by undergraduate students at one college or at a network of colleges and universities.

TELEVOTE'S IMPACT ON THE STUDENTS

First and foremost, what was the impact of the Televote process on the students who participated in it—as students, as researchers, survey designers, interviewers, analysts, and public relations experts? Anecdotally, it was my impression after running a number of these Televote courses, that the students enjoyed the entire process immensely and profited greatly from their experiences.

This is not to say that everything was ideal. When a professor conducts a course along democratic lines, giving students a great deal of power and a sense of equality in many of the class functions, there is bound to be a degree of uncertainty and chaos characterizing the situation. This makes some students very edgy and forms an environment conducive to personality conflicts and other difficulties resulting from the lack of the usual authority of the classroom structure. This occasionally occurred, detracting from some of the positive effects of the course. Nevertheless, the overall impression of the students was usually highly favorable, and from this professor's point of view, each course was an exceptional learning experience in (1) the Televote process and (2) the teaching of such a highly flexible, experiential course.

Some data from the first Televote course are exemplary. At the end of it, we asked the seventeen students who comprised the initial Televote staff to evaluate the course in a written, anonymous questionnaire. Fifteen replied, and out of that group, twelve gave the course an A and three gave it a B. Thirteen believed that Televote should become a permanent part of the political science curriculum; twelve said that the course was "among the best" or "the best" course they had ever taken at the university. Twelve noted that their general attitude toward Televote as a method of public opinion polling was "extremely favorable," while the other three rated their attitude toward Televote as "favorable." Perhaps the most telling comment, however, was a qualitative one. One student commented: "We, the students, got to see our society in real action, not in theory or the way it is supposed to work."

But what other effects did this student-facilitated interactive polling process have? After all, there were about a dozen Hawaii Televote experiments spanning eight years from 1978–85. It is true that the students who strived so diligently to make this process successful learned a great deal, but they should also be given credit for many of the accomplishments. Without their enthusiastic performances of the "sales pitch," without their persistence in convincing the Televoters that we really needed and appreciated their participation, without their determination to accumulate the proper demographic mixture, and without their zeal in promoting the results to the press, this experiment in modern participatory democracy could not have succeeded to the extent that it did. The professionalism, dedication, and altruism of hundreds of college students in an experiential democratic learning process at several universities were the proximate cause of the success of the Televote experiments.

IMPACT ON GOVERNMENT

Cynics would say that there was no way that a poll like Televote, designed and staffed by undergraduate students, could ever cause even a ripple in the halls of government. Skeptics would say that the likelihood of a ripple was minimal, at best. Idealists, in contrast, would see government rushing to use the Televote results as a guide toward widely acceptable legislation. The truth lies somewhere between the views of the skeptics and the utopians.

Who staffed and sponsored the Televote process were the major variables that determined its impact. Indeed, the most effective Televotes, in terms of influencing governmental policy, were not university based and student staffed. The Hawaii State Department of Health sponsored one Televote and staffed it with health officials. Another was sponsored by the Southern California Association of Governments and staffed by a professional polling company. In each of these cases, the results of the Televote were plugged immediately into decision-making processes and were directly related to policy changes that met with substantial public approval.

Televotes that were based in the college curriculum and that were not sponsored by a governmental entity had noticeably less impact. But that does not mean that nothing came of these efforts. In the very first experiment emanating from the Department of Political Science at the University of Hawaii, the results were actually quite dramatic. For example, whether or not to have initiative and referendum at the state level was by far the hottest topic that the 1978 state constitutional convention was about to handle. It was the major issue in the campaigns for the 102 convention seats and the principal issue that divided the delegates. As the subject of our first Televote, there was no doubt of its public importance and salience.

There had been two major polls run prior to the convention that had surveyed the people of the state on the issue of initiative and referendum. The first, about six months prior to the convention, found that about half of the voters were undecided on the issue. The second, a few months before the event, found that nearly one-third of the respondents were still unsure. Both of these surveys revealed the open secret that very few citizens knew much, if anything, about initiative and referendum—a subject rarely covered in high school civics, college courses, or the ordinary run of political campaigns.

The opponents of initiative and referendum warned of many dire consequences should the state of Hawaii write such a provision into its new constitution. But the darkest smear suggested that initiative and referendum was the darling of white, mainland intellectuals, and that the "local" folks of Hawaii—the Hawaiians, the Japanese, the Chinese, the Filipinos—were opposed to such alien notions of self-governance.

As charges and countercharges filled the air, the Televote team worked to research and print the Televote and recruit a random sample of the people of Hawaii to read it, think about it, and talk to their friends and relatives about it. The results were overwhelming!

We found that fully 86 percent of the Televoters—an excellent, representative, and well-informed sample of the people of the state—favored some form of initiative and referendum. Better yet, they were particularly impressed with indirect initiative—which had barely been mentioned in the press, in the campaigns, or during the early stages of debate at the convention. We had described the indirect initiative as part of our undisputed facts section of the Televote. This showed us that the Televoters were surely reading and thinking about the material. It was particularly interesting that racial and ethnic division disappeared. All those "locals"—the Japanese Americans, the Hawaiian Americans, the Filipino Americans—were heavily in favor of initiative and referendum.

The public relations committee prepared its news release and delivered the results to the press—as well as to the delegates of the convention—in a Televote room that we had been allotted in the same building. As luck would have it, the CBS-TV affiliate in Hawaii led off its news broadcast that night with an expose on the power clique that was controlling the convention. Members of the clique were strongly opposed to initiative and referendum but had claimed that they never held any secret meetings about it— since that was in violation of the Sunshine Laws of the state. However, the CBS camera had caught them coming out of a downtown restaurant together and highlighted that on its six o'clock news.

Right after this story, they broke the news about the Televote. They described the process in some detail and then presented the results. They played up the huge consensus in favor of initiative and referendum and then mentioned that the consensus held across all ethnic and economic groups. The clear thrust of both stories was that a small power elite in the convention was violating the law in order to oppose what the people of Hawaii overwhelmingly wanted.

The convention did not approve the initiative and referendum. So what effect did this Televote have, other than to support some vigorous investigative reporting? A number of delegates in favor of initiative employed the Televote results during the debate. In a follow-up survey after the convention, many delegates said that they were aware of the Televote and its results and thought it was a good idea for the state legislature to use it in the future.

Other impacts of the Televote were less visible. The lead professor in the Televote course was called on the telephone the day after the broadcast by the president of the convention—the leader of the opposition against initiative and referendum. He asked the faculty member to come to a well-known Waikiki restaurant the next morning for breakfast. At that time, the president conceded that the Televote had "backed us into a corner." Those in power had definitely felt the heat of informed and deliberated public opinion facilitated by undergraduate students in an experiential education course at the state university. The public had formed a deliberative judgment that they wanted to be empowered and these students had delivered the message to the media who responded quickly and effectively.

No, the Televote didn't make a big difference. Hawaii still does not have initiative and referendum at the state level. Also, the day after the breakfast meeting with the president of the convention, the lead professor was notified by the academic vice president of the University of Hawaii that he could not continue to provide extra funding for the project (for computers, long-distance telephone calls, and so forth.) "The people downtown"—as he put it—were kicking up a fuss about "politics at the university." However, he did say he would still give the Televote project his "moral support."

The New Zealand Televote offered another version of the same scenario. It was sponsored by a quasi-governmental organization known as the New Zealand Commission for the Future. Funded by Parliament, it conducted studies and projects that helped New Zealanders think about alternatives for the future of their nation. One of its major projects was a 100-page report that presented four alternative futures for New Zealand. It received a lot of media publicity and annoyed the prime minister.

The New Zealand Televote project capsulized the four scenarios into Televote form. Over one thousand randomly selected New Zealanders, recruited through the three-university Televote network, participated. Another five thousand New Zealanders participated directly by filling out Televote brochures printed in the twelve-newspaper national network. The New Zealand Radio network ran a series of talk shows on the Televote. In this fashion, the Commission's report had become very accessible and discussable, and the Televote process permitted the New Zealand public to have an informed and deliberated vote on it as well.

So what was the impact of the New Zealand Televote, aside from some consciousness-raising and increased debate over the four scenarios for the future of New Zealand? Perhaps the most immediate consequence was that it was the last straw for the prime minister. He had become a foe of the Commission for the Future, and this project bothered him a great deal because the scenario of his party had received very low support from the Televoters. Shortly afterward, the Parliament voted to relegate the Commission for the Future to history.

A few years later, the director of the Auckland University Center for the New Zealand Televote came to the East-West Center in Hawaii for a conference. We met to review the Televote process and its consequences. At that time, he was the dean of the School of Commerce at Auckland University and the research director of the leading national public opinion survey company in New Zealand. I was feeling a bit sorry about the role Televote played in the demise of the commission, but he told me that it would have met the same dismal fate even without Televote.

On the other hand, it was his view that the New Zealand Televote actually had been the harbinger of dreadful news to the prime minister and his party and that subsequent elections in New Zealand bore that out. Indeed, from his vantage point, he was surprised as to how accurately the Televote had predicted a general shift in public opinion toward a completely different set of preferences as to how the country should move into the future. He also believed that the widespread publicity about this strong sentiment had encouraged those who held this view to push it in subsequent elections.

However, the results on politics, on government, and on government policy were not always so indirect and, from the viewpoint of some, not at all negative. In two Televotes, the results were clearly direct and positive.

The 1982 Los Angeles Televote, sponsored by the Southern California Association of Governments (SCAG), dealt with several serious problems of the near future, not the least of which was how to deal with the potential horrors of hosting the 1984 Olympic Games in Los Angeles. There were many ideas floating around about how to handle security, traffic, pollution, and so forth. SCAG wanted some public discussion and input on a range of alternatives, so they decided to try the Televote process.

The Los Angeles Televote utilized much the same formula as the New Zealand Televote but had the active participation of a major Los Angeles television station as well. The process was widely publicized and the results were a clear indication as to how the member governments in SCAG should proceed. Most of the alternatives strongly supported by the Televoters were adopted and the Los Angeles Olympics were a big success. Televote played a small role in that.

It played a far bigger role in an experiment backed and funded by the state of Hawaii Department of Health (DOH) in 1985. DOH was considering a proposal to change the way it did business in a health clinic in a heavily Hawaiian community on Oahu called Waimanalo. The people at DOH had made a unilateral decision to make some drastic changes in another of their Hawaiian community programs a year or so earlier, had run into a swarm of protest, and were stung by the criticism. They felt that using the Televote process in Waimanalo might just help them avoid the same difficulties. The idea was to use the Televote to involve the people of Waimanalo in the decision-making process.

One of the biggest problems facing the Waimanalo Televote was that this process had never been used with such a low-income, poorly educated group. Would such a community participate in a project that relied so much on complex reading material? Also, being sponsored by a government agency in such a community was not necessarily a plus.

What happened was nothing short of amazing. Our recruitment rate was higher than in any previous Televote, as was the percentage of those recruited who completed the Televote. We recruited about four hundred households in a community of about two thousand five hundred households, and thus our interviewers were told that a good deal of networking was going on. Quite serendipitously, the Televote had become an instrument of increased face-to-face community deliberation. Finally, the results provided a clear direction for the DOH and ultimately they followed the lead of the community, making changes that were indicated by the Televote without much negative feedback.

CONCLUSION

We believe that the Televote experiments conclusively demonstrate it to be a method of public opinion polling that delivers what it promises: informed, deliberated, public opinion. The value to any form of democracy of such a public judgment by random samples of its citizenry should be clear.

What is more, by basing the Televote method of polling in a university curriculum as experiential education, this method is relatively inexpensive. It provides inestimable educational value to students and professors, and provides the colleges and universities with an important supportive role in community, city, state, and national affairs.

REFERENCES

Bernstein, Robert. 1989. *Elections, Representation and Congressional Voting Behavior: The Myth of Constituency Control.* Englewood Cliffs, N.J.: Prentice-Hall.
Campbell, Vincent. 1975. *Televote: A New Civic Communication System.* Palo Alto, Calif.: American Institutes for Research.
Lippmann, Walter. 1922. *Public Opinion.* New York: Harcourt Brace.

Afterword

Theodore L. Becker and Richard A. Couto

We have examined six efforts to teach democracy by being democratic: two instances of classroom practices; two instances of community-based instruction, service-learning; and two instances of developing alternative democratic practice from a university base. The next few pages explore what these efforts have in common. They do not offer a recipe or magic formula for teaching democracy or being democratic. They suggest evidence, from the efforts reported in this book, of what works in some modest way in the circumstances we have described. What we offer here are principles—necessary, we think, but not sufficient, we are aware—with which to teach democracy and to be democratic. They offer hope and direction to make our classrooms more democratic. If the lessons of these pages work in the politics of the classroom, then they may offer hope and direction to make the politics of the office, the factory, the family, and other economic and social institutions more democratic as well.

THE ART OF TEACHING DEMOCRACY

To conclude this book, we return to its origins. The editors, all but one contributor, and James MacGregor Burns participated on a panel at the American Political Science Association's 1994 annual meeting in New York. Instead of reporting a condensed version of his chapter, Richard A. Couto practiced some of the tenets of teaching democracy by being democratic. He gave his time to other panelists and to those who attended the session. He brought newsprint and magic markers and asked the participants to draw a picture of their mental picture of "teaching democracy." He borrowed this technique from Paulo Freire, the popular Brazilian educator, whom the Introduction and the first four chapters draw upon frequently. Participants then drew, literally and figuratively, from their experience and imagination.

The "data," from a 100 percent response rate, provided concise and precise images of teaching democracy. Circles were frequently used. Sometimes there was one circle representing the class and sometimes there were circles joined with one another in a circle, groups within the class. Boundaries were permeable. Teachers were not always discernible within the circles. Their permeable role boundaries permitted them to be both teachers and learners. Groups were connected to one another in class and the walls of the classroom connected the class to its campus, the surrounding community, and the social environment, providing the foundation of the roles we replicate and confront in ourselves, our small groups, and our classes.

The preceding chapters reinforce the initial findings of this reverse thematic perception test of the 1994 panel. Teaching democracy and being democratic, which are forms of transformational politics, entail changes both at the personal and the systemic levels—the classroom, the college, and the community—of which these efforts are part. The following six elements— flexible roles, democratic process, trust, commitment, construction of alternatives, and transference—make up part of the art of teaching democracy. They are common elements of the six experiences that this book has recounted and offer a starting place for teaching democracy and being democratic.

Flexible Roles

Teaching democracy and being democratic require that we accept the fluidity and frequent fluctuation and change of roles. Within a group, each member has the capacity and responsibility for leadership and teaching as well as "followership" and learning. Burns told us initially that someone has to start the action and suggested what these chapters explain: a democratic process begins changes in roles of leader and group member or teacher and student that may continue over time, a third dimension. Setting out to teach democracy by being democratic, Burns suggests, begins with the commitment to learn from the ensuing efforts and experiences and to change with those lessons.

This is not as easy as it sounds. Neither students nor teachers are blank slates upon which no one has ever written. We have been socialized to roles, many of which are undemocratic, and the more socialization we have undergone the more those roles seem to be categories with rigid behavioral expectations; boxes that are not easy to climb out of or enter into. It helps in taking on flexible roles if we, like Louis Herman, have not been totally socialized and immersed into the roles we are trying to alter or if for some other reason our vision of our goal is not impeded by the boundaries of our roles. The longer we have been socialized to roles, the more comfortable they may become, however undemocratic they may be. We can learn to live with an escape from freedom.

Authority compounds the problems of adopting flexible roles. Within our schools and institutions, teachers have unique responsibilities for the conduct of a class. In addition, we take for granted lessons from our everyday world that authority conveys power to dominate when necessary. William R. Caspary detailed the difficulties of transcending traditional forms of authority in the democratic classroom. Despite the best of intentions, students may seek an escape from the freedom of the democratic classroom and, like teachers, retreat to the certainty of lectures, the authority of the syllabus, and discussions with right and wrong answers about the material. Our insecurities stand ready to undermine our efforts. Students, as Theodore L. Becker pointed out, may get edgy in pursuing an alternative. Our alternatives and their payoffs may not always be as clear as the roles we attempt to shed.

It helps in role change to be clear about the limits of traditional roles, despite the clear demarcation of authority within them, and about the prospective improvement of flexible roles, despite the ambiguity about authority. It also helps to be clear that teaching democracy and being democratic are avenues by which to reach the democratic purpose that our colleges and universities aspire to and to challenge their actual institutional roles in social control. Granted, their democratic nature and roles may be ignored, perverted, and even partially denied, yet this simply clarifies that the problem with authority is not in the effort to create flexible roles but in the institutional tolerance of, comfort with, and defense of structures that impede the democratic nature and purpose of our institutional aspirations. There is hope for the efforts to adopt new roles. The examples we have presented have permitted teachers to meet their unique responsibilities of and for authority in new and more democratic ways.

Democratic Process

The difficulties of adopting flexible roles and confronting issues of authority within teachers and students suggest the importance of personal and social transformation. We simply can't teach democracy and be democratic with undemocratic tools. We may be tempted to keep our methods and change their content, but that won't work. As Caspary suggested, we are seeking processes to reach democratic ends—not to preach any particular means. This means investing considerably in democratic processes.

Within the discussions of this book, democratic processes take on specific meanings. They include development of self-confidence and self-esteem so that our personal needs do not intrude in or substitute for democratic process. Flexible roles with less permeable boundaries establish new personal boundaries but do not justify disregarding them. However, these roles are not new routes to old forms of racial, gender, and age discrimination. Personal interaction necessarily increases in more democratic settings, but not all personal and interpersonal boundaries dissolve because of increased interaction.

One form of interpersonal process entails storytelling; sharing our stories or personalizing the political. At the analytical level this requires making the classroom a safe space, if not a free space. At the same time, because democratic processes are interactive and reflexive in nature, sharing stories makes the classroom a safe or free space. In this, as in so many other elements of teaching and being democratic, being democratic and doing democracy become part of the same process. We do not do one thing and then another in order to become what we hope to be. Rather, we become what we want to be by doing, in the present, what we want to do when we become what we want to be.

Stories lay the foundation for sharing and interaction and are at the heart of the process of teaching and being democratic. Each instance in this book of teaching democracy and being democratic includes fostering new and more personal interaction among students and between them and other people within and beyond the classroom. Sharing stories and personalizing the political process of the classroom have their best chance to initiate a dynamic, democratic process if we keep in mind C. Wright Mills' aphorism about the sociological imagination, making private troubles into public issues, and also the insight that the women's movement provided—that the personal may be political. For example, interactive reflection on process, and the capacity to intervene to improve it, distinguished student participation in the community mediation service and the neighborhood justice center.

Democratic sharing and interaction have very specific and frequently articulated guidelines that are common to participatory and action research. Dewey's articulation of these principles are clear and concise:

- democratic citizenship in our classes requires that students respect and listen to one another
- think creatively
- arrive at creative solutions to mutual problems
- and work to implement those solutions

Implied in this process is the direct representation and full participation of each class member and the transfer of public problem-solving skills and resources. This in turn means the demystification of existing practices and the empowerment of students to affect them. We emphasized in the Introduction that little of the content of what we teach will stay with our students.

As Herman pointed out, however, our efforts to create democratic processes that build community become the personal knowledge of our students, which they value and preserve as the outcome of the democratic classroom.

Trust

Before a process of sharing and interaction can begin, someone, typically the leader, needs to establish a sufficient level of trust among those in the group. This trust extends to one another, to their mutual capacity to think creatively to identify a problem and a solution to it, and then to their own ability to work to implement that solution. Again, we find that these principles are reflexive and interactive, not linear and sequential. Involving students in the management of a significant project in a class expresses trust based on respect, rather than the results of some preceding test. Caspary points out that Dewey defined democracy by trust or "by faith in the capacity of human beings for intelligent judgment and action if proper conditions are furnished." Herman points out that mutual trust and respect undergird the Socratic premise that knowledge of the good comes from the collaborative, face to face, dialectical search for knowledge. The chapters of Parts II and III indicate what can happen for learning outcomes, community process, and democratic practices when students are trusted with and in them. On another point, grading within the aura of trust requires a focus on the ability of students rather on than their deficiencies and criticism that enables a person to develop rather than lose confidence.

Commitment

Teaching democracy and being democratic offer no shortcuts in the classroom. In fact, they offer new and more challenges to the ordinary classroom processes. It takes time and energy to pursue a process with an uncertain outcome and in the face of competing demands—our own, those of our students and our administrators, and now, in some cases, our publics. Teaching democracy and being democratic ensure uncertainty because as several of the contributors observed "questioning turns the wheel" of democracy. Questioning also turns the wheel of genuine inquiry, of course, but in lectures and in other classroom methods, teachers can use their authority to limit or structure the questions. They lose some of that control with the methods of democratic inquiry and process. Otherwise democratic values and techniques become manipulation and politics as usual. Pursuing the uncertain is exhilarating and exhausting. It will most likely require students and teachers to extend their collaboration beyond the time set aside for class. The uncertain does not function with the certainty of class hours and semesters. Rather than offering shortcuts, teaching democracy and being democratic invite us to adopt more cumbersome and less efficient processes, as

Christa Daryl Slaton did, when they enrich the deliberative and educational process.

In addition to new time management challenges, teaching democracy and being democratic foster conflict and require the commitment to resolve it. Conflict springs most naturally from differences among group members on what to do and how to do it. Once we step into the real world of media, mediation, community agencies, public officials, and others we simply invite another party to potential conflict. Conflict may offer a valuable, teachable moment in the effort to articulate, reconcile, and distinguish points of views and values. Conflict resolution and management may require more skills than a group has. More than once, the examples in this book described training in improved communication in order to reach mutual trust, group loyalty, and a sense of belonging. Caspary pointed out his own need to renew his commitment to the democratic process in the face of conflict. He reread Carl Rogers to reaffirm his belief in the intrinsic motivation of people to self-actualization. Teaching by being democratic requires not only an initial commitment to democratic process but also a renewed and increased commitment.

Other conflicts occur because of the undemocratic context our students share. Since 1972, the postindustrial society has meant more intense competition for fewer prizes. Our commitment to the greatest good for the greatest number comes at a time when economic and career opportunities appear more like the NBA draft with fewer, bigger winners and more unselected individuals left in places that underutilize their talent for lower-than-expected compensation. An emphasis on process with uncertain outcomes may foster conflict with students who resist exacerbating their uncertain futures with an uncertain present. The decline of industrial sector employment and the erosion of middle-class security provide students a context in which to apply democratic theory, as Richard Guarasci and Craig A. Rimmerman explain. The context these economic changes establish also requires a renewed commitment to democratic practice and policy and a rejection of the elitism and social divisions explicit in an economy of winners and losers reinforced by public policy. Teaching democracy by being democratic requires a commitment to develop common solutions to public problems in the community rather than to provide individual escape routes from those problems. This may invite conflicts with and among students because it requires transforming attitudes of the relation of self and society. Thus, one commitment invites conflict and conflict invites further commitment to resolve or manage it.

Obviously, the goals of teaching democracy and being democratic require more than a class and a semester. They require a commitment to learn from the process and to improve it from lessons learned. More than that, they require a commitment to reinforce the democratic processes at other times and in other places. For example, we may find ourselves called upon to assist and support other teachers in democratic innovation and our students in follow-up efforts to the work they started in class.

Construction of Alternatives

The commitment to teaching democracy and being democratic, whether in the classroom, community agencies, or university-based political innovations, entails constructing alternatives to existing practices. The cases of community mediation services and televoting are clearest and most ambitious in this emphasis. The alternative is not only external, however, but as we noted in the discussion of process, it involves transforming people— teachers and students, leaders and followers. In teaching democracy by being democratic we work to make our classroom and our society an alternative philosophical and democratic community.

Even as we depart from existing practice, it is useful to keep in mind that we bring some of it with us into the alternative. In the construction of an alternative, we maintain some elements of that which we change. Most of the cases described, for example, involved teaching methods far beyond and far more effective than simulations. Yet, like any effective simulation, these alternatives included reflection so that community service did not regress to an attitude of noblesse oblige. Likewise, improved communication skills are part of the alternative constructed by teaching democracy and being democratic, just as they are the goal of simulations. As Caspary explained and Guarasci and Rimmerman illustrated, instruction in improved communication becomes more effective when students have a felt need for it that arises "out of class experiences and struggles," that is, the effort to construct alternatives. Likewise, each of the six cases used existing mechanisms of classrooms, class assignments, and courses within the curriculum with which to construct their alternative. There are some restrictions in this process to be sure, but there are some liberating elements as well.

We do not have to achieve wholesale, institutional change before attempting innovative alternatives. We can use existing structures to accommodate new practices, an action that in itself constructs an alternative. Obviously such an alternative is unlikely to be social or institutional transformation. Few alternatives are. Those who insist on alternatives that guarantee social and institutional transformation before working on improved democratic practice have found themselves a rationale for inaction that reinforces the status quo just as rigidly as those who would defend it from change efforts. Working for democratic improvement through alternatives that fall short of total transformation makes inaction until the "right" solution comes along intolerable. Indeed, if there is a right solution for democratic transformation, it will arrive on a road traveled previously by preceding efforts at modest but important changes in democratic practice.

Transference

Transference of roles, responsibilities, and resources are implicit among these principles of teaching democracy by being democratic. Transference lies at the heart of genuine concepts of empowerment that go beyond delegation, or worse, manipulation. Transference provides the surest path to demystification of authority and the skills of critical thinking and problem solving as well. Transference and a commitment to it promote the forms of equality and imply the forms of respect that provide the foundations of community.

Transference also invokes the other principles of process and roles. The principles we offer here summarize processes that are neither unidirectional or linear. Like the fractals that illustrate change within complex systems, these processes contain systems within systems and proceed with order but not predictability. The principles of this Afterword emphasize mutual relationships and interactive and interdependent processes. Burns emphasized the principle of transference in his Foreword. Returning to that principle now underscores the relationship of these principles to one another and relates our beginning to our end.

DIFFICULT TASKS BUT WORTH THE EFFORT

We have identified a difficult set of principles. We made them more difficult by insisting on their interdependence: They invite teachers to adopt new roles; to change authority relationships; to undertake personal transformation; and to accept increased risks for conflict and uncertainty. These are not easy tasks, and we do not suggest that they are. We assert only that they can be undertaken and that they are worth the effort because they may make us better and more effective teachers. They are worth the effort also because they sustain our hope for a democratic politics of increased justice, peace, and equality and direct us to a path we can travel with our students to reach increased and improved democratic practice.

Bibliography

BOOKS

Alper, Benedict and Lawrence Nichols. 1981. *Beyond the Courtroom: Programs in Community Justice and Conflict Resolution*. Lexington, Mass.: Lexington Books.

Anzaldua, Gloria. 1987. *Borderlands: The New Mestiza-La Frontera*. New York: Aunt Lute Books.

Argyris, Chris, Robert Putnam, and Diana McLain Smith. 1985. *Action Science*. San Francisco: Jossey-Bass Publishers.

Barber, Benjamin R. 1984. *Strong Democracy: Participatory Politics for a New Age*. Berkeley: University of California Press.

———. 1992. *An Aristocracy of Everyone: The Politics of Education and the Future of America*. New York: Ballantine Books.

Bellah, Robert N., Richard Madsen, William M. Sullivan, Ann Swindler, and Steven M. Tipton. 1985. *Habits of the Heart: Individualism and Commitment in American Life*. Berkeley: University of California Press.

Bernstein, Richard. 1983. *Beyond Objectivism and Relativism: Science, Hermeneutics, and Praxis*. Philadelphia: University of Pennsylvania Press.

Bernstein, Robert. 1989. *Elections, Representation and Congressional Voting Behavior: The Myth of Constituency Control*. Englewood Cliffs, N.J.: Prentice-Hall.

Bonwell, Charles and James A. Eison. 1991. *Active Learning: Creating Excitement in the Classroom*. Washington, D.C.: ASHE-ERIC Higher Education Report No. 1.

Boyer, Ernest. 1987. *College: The Undergraduate Experience in America*. New York: Harper & Row.

Boydston, J., ed. 1981–1992. *John Dewey: The Later Works: 1925–1953.* Carbondale, Ill.: Southern Illinois University Press.

Boyte, Harry C. 1980. *The Backyard Revolution.* Philadelphia: Temple University Press.

Burns, James MacGregor. 1978. *Leadership.* New York: Harper & Row.

Campbell, Vincent. 1975. *Televote: A New Civic Communication System.* Palo Alto, Calif.: American Institutes for Research.

Coles, Robert. 1993. *The Call to Service: A Witness to Idealism.* Boston: Houghton Mifflin.

Couto, Richard A. 1982. *Streams of Idealism and Health Care Innovation: An Assessment of Service-Learning and Community Mobilization.* New York: Teachers College Press, Columbia University.

Dewey, John. 1916. *Essays in Experimental Logic.* Chicago: University of Chicago Press.

Dionne, E. J., Jr. 1991. *Why Americans Hate Politics.* New York: Simon and Schuster.

Dye, Thomas R. and Harmon Zeigler. 1996. *The Irony of Democracy.* 10th ed. Belmont, Calif.: Wadsworth Publishing Co.

Fay, Brian. 1987. *Critical Social Science: Liberation and Its Limits.* Ithaca, N.Y.: Cornell University Press.

Freire, Paulo. 1970. *Pedagogy of the Oppressed.* New York: Continuum Publishing Co.
———. 1973. *Education for Critical Consciousness.* New York: Continuum Publishing Co.

Gamson, Zelda F. and Associates. 1984. *Liberating Education.* San Francisco: Jossey-Bass.

Gandhi, M. 1951. *Nonviolent Resistance.* New York: Schocken Books.

Gaventa, John. 1980. *Power and Powerlessness: Quiescence and Rebellion in an Appalachian Valley.* Urbana: University of Illinois Press.

Glen, John. 1988. *Highlander: No Ordinary School, 1932–1962.* Lexington: University Press of Kentucky.

Gorham, Eric B. 1992. *National Service Citizenship and Political Education.* Albany: State University of New York Press.

Greider, William. 1992. *Who Will Tell the People: The Betrayal of American Democracy.* New York: Simon and Schuster.

Hacker, Andrew. 1992. *Two Nations: Black and White, Separate, Hostile, Unequal.* New York: Scribner's.

Harwood Group, The. 1991. *Citizens and Politics: A View from Main Street America.* Dayton, Ohio: The Kettering Foundation.

Horkheimer, Max. 1972. *Critical Theory, The Social Function of Philosophy.* New York: Seabury Press.
———. 1974. *The Eclipse of Reason.* New York: Seabury Press. 1974.

Johansen, Bruce E. 1982. *The Forgotten Founders: How the American Indian Helped Shape Democracy.* Boston: Harvard Common Press.

Jung, Carl G. 1973. *Mandala Symbolism.* Princeton: Princeton University Press.

Kolb, David A. 1984. *Experiential Learning: Experience as the Source of Learning and Development.* Englewood Cliffs, N.J.: Prentice-Hall.

Kuhn, Thomas. 1970. *The Structure of Scientific Revolutions.* 2nd ed. Chicago: University of Chicago Press.

Kupiec, Tamar Y., ed. 1993. *Rethinking Tradition: Integrating Service with Academic Study on College Campuses.* Providence, R.I.: Campus Compact.

Levine, Arthur. 1980. *When Dreams and Heroes Died.* San Francisco: Jossey-Bass.

Lincoln, Yvonne S. and Egon G. Guba. 1985. *Naturalistic Inquiry.* Beverly Hills, Calif.: Sage.

Lindbloom, Charles E. 1990. *Inquiry and Change: The Troubled Attempt to Understand and Shape Society.* New Haven: Yale University Press.

—— and David Cohen. 1976. *Usable Knowledge.* New Haven: Yale University Press.

Lippmann, Water. 1922. *Public Opinion.* New York: Harcourt Brace.

Lorde, Audre. *Sister Outsider.* Freedom, Calif.: The Crossing Press Feminist Series.

McGills, Daniel. 1978. *Neighborhood Justice Centers.* Washington, D.C.: Government Printing Office.

Miller, Anne. 1981. *The Drama of the Gifted Child.* New York: Basic Books.

Newman, Frank. 1985. *Higher Education and the American Resurgence.* Princeton, N.J.: Carnegie Foundation for the Advancement of Teaching.

Parenti, Michael. 1983. *Democracy for the Few.* 4th ed. New York: St. Martin's Press.

Paul, Richard. 1990. *Critical Thinking: What Every Person Needs to Survive in a Rapidly Changing World.* Sonoma, Calif.: Sonoma State University, Center for Critical Thinking.

Plato. 1938. *Portrait of Socrates, being the Apology, Crito and Phaedo of Plato in an Englishs Translation.* Edited by Richard Livingstone. Oxford: The Clarendon Press.

Rimmerman, Craig A. 1993. *Presidency by Plebiscite: The Reagan-Bush Era in Institutional Perspective.* Boulder, Colo.: Westview Press.

Rogers, Carl. 1961. *On Becoming a Person: A Therapist's View of Psychotherapy.* Boston: Houghton Mifflin.

Rousseau, Jean-Jacques. 1950. *The Social Contract.* 1762; New York: Dutton.

Schott, Cheryl. 1994. *COMPS: Community Problem Solving Seminar Handbook.* Richmond: University of Richmond, LINCS Program.

Shor, Ira and Paulo Freire. 1987. *A Pedagogy for Liberation: Dialogues on Transforming Education.* New York: Bergin & Garvey.

Storm, Hyemeyohsts. 1972. *Seven Arrows.* New York: Harper and Row.

Terkel, Studs. 1992. *Race.* New York: New Press.

Vlastos, Gregory. 1991. *Socrates: Ironist and Moral Philosopher.* Ithaca, N.Y.: Cornell University Press.

Warhaftig, Paul, ed. 1977. *The Citizen Dispute Resolution Handbook.* Pittsburgh, Pa.: Middle Atlantic Region, American Friends Service Committee.

Wilson, William J. 1987. *The Truly Disadvantaged: The Inner City, the Underclass and Public Policy.* Chicago: University of Chicago Press.

Winter, David G., D. C. McClelland, and A. J. Stewart. 1981. *A New Case for the Liberal Arts: Assessing Institutional Goals and Student Development.* San Francisco: Jossey-Bass.

ARTICLES AND BOOK CHAPTERS

Alpert, Eugene. 1987. "The Internship Journal: Can Academic Quality Be Maintained?" Paper presented at the annual meeting of the American Political Science Association. Chicago, Illinois.

Astin, Alexander. 1987. "Competition or Cooperation." *Change* (September/October): 12-19.

Bandow, Doug. 1993. "National Service: Utopias Revisited." *Policy Analysis*. The Cato Institute 190 (March 15): 1-15.

Barber, Benjamin R. 1992a. "Going to the Community." *The Civic Arts Review* 5, no. 4 (Fall): 10-12.

———— and Richard Battistoni. 1993. "A Season of Service: Introducing Service Learning into the Liberal Arts Curriculum." *PS: Political Science & Politics* 26, no. 2 (June): 235-40.

Barnes, C. P. 1983. "Questioning in College Classrooms." In C. L. Ellner and C. P. Barnes, *Studies of College Teaching*, 61-81. Lexington, Mass.: Lexington Books. Quoted in James Eison, Fred Janzow, and Charles Bonwell, 1990.

Boyte, Harry C. 1991a. "Community Service and Civic Education." *Phi Delta Kappan* (June): 765-67.

————. 1991b. "Turning on Youth to Politics." *The Nation* (May 13): 626-28.

————. 1993. "What is Citizenship Education?" In *Rethinking Tradition: Integrating Service with Academic Study on College Campuses*, ed. Tamar Y. Kupiec, 63-66. Providence, R.I.: Campus Compact.

Couto, Richard A. 1987. "Participatory Research: Methodology and Critique." *The Clinical Sociology Review* 5: 83-90.

————. 1990. "Assessing a Community Setting as a Context for Learning." In *Combining Service and Learning: A Resource Book for Community and Public Service*, vol. 2, ed. Jane C. Kendall, 251-66. Raleigh, N.C.: National Society for Internships and Experiential Education.

————. 1993. "Service Learning in Service to Leadership Studies." In *Rethinking Tradition: Integrating Service with Academic Study on College Campuses*, ed. Tamar Y. Kupiec, 67-71. Providence, R.I.: Campus Compact.

Dewey, John. 1939. "Creative Democracy." In *John Dewey: The Political Writings*, ed. D. Morris and I. Shapiro. Indianapolis: Hackett Publishing Company.

Eison, James A., Fred Janzow, and Charles Bonwell. 1990. "Active Learning Development Workshops: Or Practicing What We Teach." *The Journal of Staff, Program and Organization Development* 5, no. 2 (Summer).

Harkavy, Ira. 1993. "University-Community Partnerships: The University of Pennsylvania and West Philadelphia as a Case Study." In *Rethinking Tradition: Integrating Service with Academic Study on College Campuses*, ed. Tamar Y. Kupiec, 121-28. Providence, R.I.: Campus Compact.

Honnet, Ellen Porter and Susan J. Poulsen. 1989. "Principles of Good Practice for Combining Service and Learning." *The Wingspread Journal: Special Report*. Racine, Wisc.: The Johnson Foundation, Inc.

Hursh, Barbara. 1990. "Tools for Journals and Debriefing." In *Combining Service and Learning: A Resource Book for Community and Public Service*, vol. 2, ed. Jane C. Kendall, 80-86. Raleigh, N.C.: National Society for Internships and Experiential Education.

Kuhn, Thomas. 1977. "Objectivity, Values, and Theory Choice." In *The Essential Tension*. Chicago: University of Chicago Press.

Lawry, John D. 1990. "Caritas in the Classroom: The Opening of the American Student's Heart." *College Teaching* 38, no. 3 (Summer): 83-87.

McKeachie, Wilbert. 1990. "Research on College Teaching: The Historical Background." *Journal of Educational Psychology* 82, no. 2: 189-200.

Park, Peter. 1992. "The Discovery of Participatory Research as a New Scientific Paradigm: Personal and Intellectual Accounts." *The American Sociologist* (Winter): 29-42.

Rodabaugh, Rita. 1994. "In the Name of the Student." *Teaching Excellence* 6, no. 3.

Rowe, M. B. 1974a. "Pausing Phenomena; Influence on the Quality of Instruction." *Journal of Psycholinguistic Research* 3: 203-24(a). Quoted in James Eison, Fred Janzow, and Charles Bonwell, 1990.

————. 1974b. "Wait-time and Rewards as Instructional Variables." *Journal of Research in Science Teaching* 11: 81-94. Quoted in James Eison, Fred Janzow, and Charles Bonwell, 1990.

Stanton, Timothy. 1981. "Discovering the Ecology of Human Organizations: Exercises for Field Study Students." In *Field Study: A Source Book for Experiential Learning*, ed. Lenore Borzak. Beverly Hills, Calif.: Sage Publications.

Zimmerman, Jane, Vicki Zawacki, Jan Bird, Virginia Peterson, and Charles Norman. 1990. "Journals: Diaries for Growth." In *Combining Service and Learning: A Resource Book for Community and Public Service*, vol. 2, ed. Jane C. Kendall, 69-79. Raleigh, N.C.: National Society for Internships and Experiential Education.

Index

Action research, 96–97, 100–101, 122, 152, 166
Active learning, 56, 58; strategies of, 65
Alternatives, creating, 76, 169
American higher education, 13–14, 17–18, 20, 26, 53; and community service, 81–82, 87, 136; and the market, 57
Anzaldua, Gloria, 113
Appalachian Student Health Coalition, 80–81
Assignments, 27; self-directed learning, 29–34
Authority: changes in, 99; questioning, 4, 5, 6, 19, 34, 36; and roles, 165; teachers as, 32, 42–43, 50–51, 56, 61; training to obey, 11, 45

Bandow, Doug, 108
Barber, Benjamin, 18, 19, 85, 101, 117
Becker, Theodore L., 54, 122, 165
Bell, Griffin, 123
Bellah, Robert, 110
Boyte, Harry C., 18, 101, 106, 116
Burns, James MacGregor, 3, 93, 163, 164

Cambell, Vincent, 148
Campus Compact, 17, 81
Campus Outreach Opportunity League (COOL), 17
Caspary, William R., 54, 165, 167, 168, 169
Center for Health Services. *See* Vanderbilt University
Civic education, 18, 85, 98–99, 101, 102, 105–6, 109, 112; and political autobiography, 113–15
Classroom discussion, 41, 54, 58, 62, 72, 82. *See also* Group process; Group work; Medicine wheel; Quality circle; Socratic method
Coles, Robert, 109, 113
Communication, 41–42, 168, 169
Community, viii; of need and response, viii, 85–87; search for, 53, 59, 100. *See also* Transformation; Transformational politics
Community Mediation Service (CMS), 123, 126–30, 169; and apprenticeship model, 133–35; and change, 124, 137–41; policies of, 130–32
Community organizations, 3, 83; and

About the Editors and Contributors

THEODORE L. BECKER is Professor of Political Science at Auburn University. He received the Distinguished Career Award from the American Political Science Association's Section on Transformational Politics in 1995. Among his many publications is the recently published *Quantum Politics* (Praeger 1991). His work on televoting now extends to cyberspace. His website, Teledemocracy Action News Network can be found at http://www.auburn.edu/~tann.

JAMES MACGREGOR BURNS continues his distinguished career at Williams College where he is Woodrow Wilson Professor of Government Emeritus. He has served as president of the American Political Science Association. Presently, he divides his time between Williamstown and the Center for Political Leadership and Participation at the University of Maryland. His current research includes a revision of his seminal 1978 book, *Leadership*.

WILLIAM R. CASPARY is Associate Professor of Political Science at Washington University (St. Louis). He is working on a book on John Dewey's theory of participatory democracy and has published research on the causes of war. He has worked as an ombudsman, mediator, educational consultant, and square-dance fiddler.

RICHARD A. COUTO is Professor of Leadership Studies at the Jepson School of the University of Richmond. His book on civil rights, *Lifting the*

Veil, received the award for best book in transformational politics in 1994 from the American Political Science Association. He is currently completing a book on mediating structures, social capital, and democratic theory.

RICHARD GUARASCI is Dean of Hobart College and Professor of Political Science. He has written on democratic theory and citizenship as well as higher education. His latest book on democracy, intercultural citizenship, and higher education, *The Good College,* will be published in 1997.

LOUIS HERMAN is Assistant Professor and Head of the Political Science Program at the University of Hawaii, West Oahu. His current research addresses both political inquiry and political theory. He received the University of Hawaii Board of Regents' medal and prize for excellence in teaching and the Outstanding Professor award from University of Hawaii West Oahu Student Government.

CRAIG A. RIMMERMAN is Associate Professor of Political Science at Hobart and William Smith Colleges. He served as an American Political Science Association congressional fellow in 1992-93. He is the author of *Presidency by Plebiscite* (1996) and editor of *Gay Rights, Military Wrongs* (1993). He is currently working on a book that examines the relationship between democracy, participation, community service, and the new citizenship in American politics.

CHRISTA DARYL SLATON is Associate Professor of Political Science at Auburn University. She coordinated the American Political Science Association Section on Transformational Politics from 1993 to 1995. She authored *Televote: Expanding Citizen Participation in the Quantum Age* (Praeger 1992) and is coauthoring a forthcoming book on transformational politics.

ISBN 0-275-95552-4

90000>

EAN

9 780275 955526

HARDCOVER BAR CODE